The Best Ground in the Fourt

A History of Burnley Football Clu
Andrew Procter

This is the week-to-week story of ⸻g ⸻ period
of its greatest triumphs and, ultimately, its saddest decline. The story
of a club travelling the bumpy road from international renown to
near-obscurity with all the ups and downs that can be imagined in
between.

The reader is given all the information he needs to judge for himself
why Burnley should have plummetted from first in Division One
to last in Division Four in 27 years. Was money spent on ground
improvements at the expense of success on the field of play? Or can
Burnley's fall be linked with the abolition of the maximum wage in
the early sixties; the sale of too many good and influential players;
the reign of Bob Lord; the appointment of an 'outside' manager? Or
was it all part of the general decline of Lancashire town clubs during
the period?

The facts are presented as they unfold from season to season, so that
anyone interested in a particular Burnley team, or a particular season
or group of seasons, will be fully informed regarding playing success,
transfers and any other important events connected with the club.
They will be able to get a feel, too, of the hopes and fears of Burnley
fans during the period.

The story is presented in such a way that events, especially those on
the field, are allowed to tell their own tale. Each reader can make up
his or her own mind about Burnley Football Club. They do so under
the guidance of an author who is able to present every event in a
detached and non-partisan way, and yet who writes with the author-
ity and sensitivity of one who has been deeply involved with the
club during this period.

THE BEST GROUND IN THE FOURTH DIVISION

A History of Burnley Football Club
(1960–1988)

Andrew Procter

JANUS PUBLISHING COMPANY
London, England

First published in Great Britain 1992 by
Janus Publishing Company

© Andrew Procter 1991

**British Library Cataloguing-in-
Publication Data.
A catalogue record for this book
is available from the British Library.**

ISBN 1 85756 010 8

Cover design David Murphy
Cover photograph courtesy The Burnley Express
Printed in Great Britain by
View Publications (Bristol) Limited

Contents

INTRODUCTION   vii

AT THE TOP
(2 May 1960–16 January 1963)   1

NEAR THE TOP
(26 January 1963–18 April 1967)   13

THE FOURTEENTH BEST TEAM IN ENGLAND
(April 1967–May 1970)   27

'THE TEAM OF THE SEVENTIES'
(May 1970–10 June 1975)   35

INTERNAL DECLINE
(16 August 1975–12 April 1980)   53

INDIAN SUMMER
(May 1980–2 June 1983)   67

JOHN BOND AND AFTER
(14 June 1983–9 May 1987)   77

THE ROAD TO WEMBLEY
(10 May 1987–29 May 1988)   90

Introduction

'Do we want a successful side or the best ground in the Fourth Division?' was a rhetorical question asked in the local press in August 1975 following the sale of Martin Dobson to Everton for £300,000. Ten years later, it may not have been what most people wanted, but Burnley Football Club had achieved the latter objective.

Was the rapid decline in Burnley's playing fortunes a direct result of the ground redevelopment, or were other factors involved? How could a club so successfully run in the 1960s have reached such a lowly position in the football world? This book charts that decline – from the zenith of winning the Championship in 1960 to the nadir of nearly losing Football League status at the end of the 1986–87 season.

Many reasons have been put forward for this decline: the abolition of the maximum wage; the sale of Jimmy McIlroy; the reign of Bob Lord; the appointment of John Bond. Other suggestions saw it in its wider context – as merely another part of the general decline of the Lancashire town clubs. A comparison of the First Divisions of 1960 and 1987 shows the replacement of Blackburn Rovers, Preston North End, Blackpool and Bolton Wanderers by Watford, Norwich City, Wimbledon and Luton Town. Nevertheless, the fortunes of the Lancashire teams have taken widely divergent paths and so purely footballing matters must be taken into consideration.

The demise of Burnley as a footballing force is all the more sad because of the club's long and illustrious history. Formed in 1882, the club was one of the founder members of the Football League 6 years later. After 30 undistinguished and largely unsuccessful years, Burnley created a very good team around World War One. The FA Cup was won in 1914, and the Championship 7 years later. But for the war, the team could have been more successful – its quality can be seen in the record-breaking 30-match undefeated run in the Championship-winning 1920–21 season.

The club had to wait until after World War Two for more success. In 1947, the team won promotion from Division Two and reached the FA˙ Cup Final, losing narrowly to Charlton Athletic. This side, which finished third in its first season in Division One, laid the foundation for an unbroken run of twenty-four years in the top flight.

In the 1950s, Burnley finished in the top six on two occasions, but did not mount a serious challenge for the title until the 1959–60 campaign. The Championship had been in the possession of Wolverhampton Wanderers for the previous two seasons, and it was they who led the Championship race until the very last moment. Burnley had to win their last game, which was against Manchester City. In an evening kick-off at Maine Road, Burnley took the lead through Brian Miller, but this goal was pegged back by City's Joe Hayes. This meant that Trevor Meredith's goal clinched the game, and took Burnley to the top of the league for the first time that season. It was the only time that mattered – Burnley were Champions of England.

The final match of the 1986–87 season saw the Clarets attempting to stave off relegation from Division Four and only a battling performance and another 2–1 victory – against Orient on 9 May 1987 – in the final game saved the club from this fate. The size of the crowd for this match (17,600) was around six times the season's average, and reflected the widespread concern for Burnley's plight. The immense amount of publicity that surrounded that game can only be explained in the context of the club's former status as one of the elite of British football. Mentioning to people that you are from Burnley will often provoke the response, 'They used to have a football team, didn't they?' and the mention of such names as Jimmy McIlroy, Ralph Coates, Martin Dobson, Leighton James and Trevor Steven. But ask them to name any of the current squad, and they will be hard pressed to do so.

To most people, Burnley Football Club in the 1990s is just another struggling lower division team. Talk of the Premier League does not involve the club, but it was not always so. In the 1960s it would have been unthinkable to leave Burnley out of such plans. To its own supporters, however, the club retains an immense importance. In Burnley, the Football Club is a vital part of the town's identity. Recent lack of success has done little to diminish this position, and only serves to emphasise its significance.

This almost tribal loyalty has made Turf Moor not only the best ground in the Fourth Division, but also the best attended. For the past three seasons, Burnley's gates have been consistently the highest in Division Four, often exceeding some in Division One.

Unfortunately, the quality of football has done little to justify such attendances. Since the trip to Wembley in 1988, little progress has been made on the field of play. Whilst never being in any danger of relegation from Division Four, promotion has not yet been achieved. The play-offs were reached in 1990–91 season, but a disappointing result at Torquay put paid to hopes of another trip to Wembley for the play-off finals and a possible place in Division Three. The 1991–92 season has begun well and it is to be hoped that it will continue to be successful, but ambitions of recapturing former glories must still lie a long way in the future.

There is no reason to believe that Burnley will not be successful again, but it would be a great shame if the impetus gained in 1987 and 1988 is lost. Success needs to be achieved soon if the club is not to sink back into the torpor of the mid–1980s. Even the most ardent supporter will find yet another season in Division Four hard to take.

It is to be hoped that the recent appointment of Jimmy Mullen as manager can provide the necessary impetus so that Burnley FC can once again fulfil its potential and write another chapter of achievement in its eventful and varied history.

Chapter 1

At the Top

(2 May 1960–16 January 1963)

For 3 years Burnley remained a major footballing force in the country, without actually adding any more honours to the Championship of 1959–60 (except for a 6-month share of the 1960 Charity Shield). On 16 January 1963, Burnley defeated their main rivals, Tottenham Hotspur, in an ill-tempered FA Cup tie. Spurs had been the cup-holders for the previous two seasons, and had beaten Burnley in the latter stages of both campaigns. This victory, at a snow-covered White Hart Lane, seemed to clear the way for another successful season, but in retrospect, it appears to mark the last great achievement of that Burnley squad.

None of the squad had previously played for any other English league club – the Burnley success being very much home-produced. Goalkeeper, Adam Blacklaw, a Scot, missed only one league game during this period. He had made his debut in 1956, but started a prolonged run only after the injury to the England international, Colin MacDonald in 1959. Blacklaw was joined by the young full-back partnership of John Angus and Alex Elder, both full internationals. Angus won his only England cap in 1961 against Austria, whilst Elder, who had been signed from Glentoran in 1959, was a regular member of the Northern Ireland team.

The half-back line had more experience. Centre-half, Tommy Cummings had made his debut in 1948, 3 years before that of Jimmy Adamson, the club skipper. Brian Miller, left half, was another England international (like Angus, his only appearance was in Vienna in 1961). Right-half, Walter Joyce made 30 Division One appearances in the 1960–61 season, but failed to establish his place the following year. The eventual successor to Cummings was John Talbut, who became a regular member of the team in August 1962.

Up front, John Connelly, the outside right, was the only Burnley player to be selected for the 1962 World Cup in Chile (except for

Adamson, who was chosen as assistant to England manager, Walter Winterbottom. Adamson could have been Winterbottom's successor, but declined the post, leaving the way clear for Alf Ramsey).

Jimmy McIlroy was widely regarded as one of the best inside-forwards in Britain. He won over 50 caps for Northern Ireland and made his Burnley debut in 1950. Like Elder, some years later, McIlroy was obtained from Glentoran. Ray Pointer, who earned three England caps, was the club's regular centre forward until September 1962, when he moved to the inside right position to make room for the young Scot, Andy Lochhead. He, in turn, replaced regular inside left, Jimmy Robson, who was leading scorer in the 1960–61 season with 25 goals. Along with Adamson, Cummings, Angus, Pointer, Talbut and manager, Harry Potts, he made up a strong Geordie contingent in the Burnley squad. In 1960, the left wing position was in the possession of Brian Pilkington, who had been with the club since 1952, and played his one game for England in 1955. Early in 1961, he was replaced by Gordon Harris, a player signed from Frickley Colliery, who had made his debut in 1959.

The club also boasted a very strong reserve team, including goalkeeper Jim Furnell; Colne-born half back, David Walker; Trevor Meredith (who scored the Championship-winning goal in 1960); Ian Lawson, who scored four goals on his debut in 1957; and 'McIlroy's deputy', Ronnie Fenton. The quality of the first team left few opportunities for these talented reserves and many had to leave for other clubs to obtain first team football.

This produced a regular income for the club. £34,000 was obtained in February 1962 for the sale of Jim Furnell and Ian Lawson to Liverpool and Leeds United respectively. The reserve team full back and captain, Billy Marshall was transferred to Oldham Athletic the following August for £5,000 and 3 months later, Ronnie Fenton went to West Bromwich Albion for £17,000. At a time when £100,000 players were a rarity, the sale of four reserves for £56,000 was an admirable piece of business.

During the same period, no moves were made to strengthen the squad. Great faith was placed in the youth policy that had produced the Championship-winning side and that was expected to carry on producing players of the same quality. Money had already been spent on the training ground at Gawthorpe. The land had been purchased by Bob Lord, the Burnley chairman, in January 1955 for £5,250 and a further £30,000 was spent on the construction of a gymnasium at Turf Moor in 1962. Burnley was the first football club to possess such facilities, which gave it a head start in nourishing the young talent found by its expansive scouting network. It cannot be denied that the youth policy was an invaluable factor in Burnley's success, but perhaps an over-reliance on its potential and a subsequent refusal to buy limited this success. Bob Lord's *idee fixe* of the youth policy made for an extremely successful small town club, but never anything more.

The chairman refused to contemplate spending money on the team, but in September 1961, he unveiled plans for a grandiose L-shaped stand for the Bee Hole End and Brunshaw Road side of the ground. It would seat 17,000 and cost £200,000, which Lord believed could be met out of club profits. He also had plans for the reorganisation of football, with a British League of two divisions, and the remainder of clubs in regional leagues. The only victim of his scheme was Accrington Stanley. In January 1962, Lord was called in to advise on Accrington's financial difficulties and he thought that they should learn their 'proper place in football. They would gain more in the Lancashire Combination than in the Football League.' There seems little doubt, judging by the lack of subsequent withdrawals, that Accrington's place could have been saved, and while no aspersions should be cast over Lord's sincerity, his advice was most certainly misplaced. All Accrington's fixtures were cancelled – the first consequence of which was that Burnley received a bye in the Lancashire Senior Cup. Lord's overriding concern was with Burnley Football Club and this could lead to strained relations with the press. During the 1960–61 season, for example, the correspondents of both the *Burnley Express* and the *Daily Mail* were banned from the Turf Moor press box. 'Victims of his disapproval,' one magazine claimed, 'must feel as if they have been clouted across the mazzard with the carcass of an ox.' But Bob Lord always did what he thought right for the club, and the club's success during this period cannot be denied.

Before the start of the 1960–61 season, the club announced a profit of £13,654 10s 7d for the year, which left a credit balance of £57,190 12s 5d. Season ticket sales brought in £29,565 and it was therefore possible to retain 41 players for the new season.

The team that opened the season on 13 August 1960 against Wolves in the FA Charity Shield at Turf Moor was:

Blacklaw

Angus   Elder

Adamson   Cummings   Miller

Connelly   McIlroy   Pointer   Robson   Pilkington

Goals by Miller and Connelly earned the Clarets a draw, and the Shield was held for 6 months by both clubs. The first league game of the season against Arsenal at Turf Moor resulted in a 3–2 home win, but the good start was not maintained. Burnley twice went down to Manchester City within a week, and further defeats by Cardiff City and Sheffield Wednesday led to manager, Harry Potts, making changes. Tommy Cummings was replaced by Walter Joyce, who came in at right half (Adamson moving over to centre half). The return of John Connelly after eight games out with injury helped Burnley to a 5–0 win against Fulham (Jimmy Robson got a hat-trick, Ray Pointer the others) and in October, the Clarets rose to third place with impressive victories at Blackburn Rovers (4–1), Chelsea (6–2 – another Robson hat-trick) and at Turf Moor against Manchester United (5–3). But with Tottenham in virtually unbeatable form in the league the major events of the season occurred in the various cup competitions.

As Champions, Burnley qualified for the European Cup and received a bye in the first round. In the second, they were drawn against the French Champions, Rheims, whose squad included the French internationals, Raymond Kopa and Juste Fontaine. The latter was the leading scorer in the previous World Cup competition. In the previous ten seasons Rheims had been French champions on four occasions and had appeared in two European Cup finals. Fontaine was injured and thus missed the first leg at Turf Moor on 16 November 1960. Burnley had warmed up well with a 5–3 win over Wolves the previous Saturday. In front of a crowd of 36,742, Burnley took a two-goal advantage to the second leg, through goals by Robson and McIlroy. The second leg, played at the Park de Princes in Paris in the hope of attracting a larger crowd, produced a stormy match. At one stage, Harry Potts ran on to the field to attempt to prevent the Rheims players moving forward a free-kick. As a result of this action, he was subsequently banned from the touchline for the remainder of the season (he had already been officially warned following remarks to the referee in a match on Burnley's summer tour of the USA). Even the presence of Fontaine was not enough for the French Champions. He afterwards proclaimed Blacklaw to be the best goalkeeper in Europe and although Burnley were beaten 3–2 on the night, they went through on aggregate. In the next round, they were drawn against Hamburg SV, the German Champions, who were once again top of their league, having dropped only one point all season.

The first leg against Hamburg played in January 1961 before a Turf Moor crowd of 46,000 proved a great cause for optimism when Burnley went three goals up, through two by Brian Pilkington and one from Robson. Dorpel pulled one back for Hamburg but it seemed that Burnley could progress in this tournament, as in the other cup competitions.

In October (1960), Burnley competed in the newly-inaugurated Football League Cup. The second round game at Cardiff allowed Burnley to field some of the reserves: Billy Marshall; Jimmy Scott; Ronnie Fenton; and Gordon Harris, who scored three of the team's four goals. Several of the other top clubs (Arsenal, Wolves, Sheffield Wednesday, Spurs and West Brom) had decided not to enter the new competition fearing fixture congestion at the end of the season. Bearing in mind Burnley's extra European commitments, the decision to compete was unwise, and league form appears to have been affected.

Tottenham were running away with the Championship, and when the two teams met at White Hart Lane in December, Spurs raced into a four-goal lead, but goals by Connelly(2), Robson and Pointer earned a point for the Clarets in a memorable game. Good wins against Arsenal (5–2) and Newcastle United (5–3) placed Burnley in third position at the turn of the year, but they were now 13 points behind Tottenham.

The third round League Cup tie at Brentford was scheduled for just before the second clash with Rheims. The club, therefore, decided to field its reserve side, much to the chagrin of the 9,900 crowd at Griffin Park. Nevertheless, the reserves acquitted themselves well and an Andy Lochhead goal 7 minutes from time forced a replay at Turf Moor. One reason given for fielding a weakened Burnley team was that four of the regulars (Angus, Blacklaw, Connelly and Robson) were working out their notices with the National Coal Board, and they did not begin full-time training until the following week.

Part-time players were by no means unusual before the abolition of the £20 maximum wage in 1961. Nonetheless, the club was warned for fielding a sub-strength team, but this did not stop it fielding a similar side against Chelsea on the Saturday before the European Cup tie in Hamburg. The Burnley team on 11 March 1961 read:

Furnell

Smith   Marshall

Walker   Talbut   Scott

Meredith   Lawson   Lochhead   Fenton   Harris

Only a late goal by Jimmy Greaves prevented a famous victory for the young side, but despite the 4–4 scoreline, the club was fined £1,000 by the Football League Management Committee.

Not even a rested full-strength side could resist Hamburg in the second leg. Brian Pilkington, the scorer of two goals in the first game had lost his place in the team to Gordon Harris in February, and had been transferred to Bolton Wanderers for £25,000. It was Harris's goal, a stunning 20-yard effort just after half-time that renewed hope for the fans in England, where the game was being televised live. Hamburg had levelled the aggregate score by the break and after Harris' goal they scored twice more to run out 4–1 winners (5–4 on aggregate). The Germans, inspired by captain Uwe Seeler (scorer of two of the goals) and a crowd of 71,000 had proved unstoppable. The small Lancashire club had acquitted itself splendidly in Europe, and it still maintained an interest in both domestic cup competitions.

Progress had been made into the semi-finals of both the FA Cup and the League Cup. In the league, the first home victory of the year did not come until the last day of March, whereas in the FA Cup, victories over Bournemouth, Brighton and Hove Albion (after a replay), Swansea City and Sheffield Wednesday (also after two games) led to a semi-final against Tottenham Hotspur at Villa Park. Circumstances were not in favour of the Clarets – the tie was only 3 days after the match in Hamburg, against a team in almost invincible form, on a ground where Burnley had not won since 1950. The game itself was a great disappointment to the Burnley followers in the 70,000 crowd the team falling to a Bobby Smith hat-trick. (A measure of revenge was gained later in the season, when Spurs, already

Champions, were defeated 4–2 at Turf Moor – hence, Burnley obtained three points and eight goals from the illustrious double-winning side).

In the League Cup, victories over Cardiff City, Brentford, Nottingham Forest and Southampton set up a two-legged semi-final with Aston Villa. Both legs resulted in draws (1–1 at Turf Moor, 2–2 at Villa Park) and in the decider at Old Trafford, Burnley were without McIlroy and Elder on international duty, and went down 2–1 to a late goal from Gerry Hitchens. Two semi-finals, European Cup quarter finals and fourth in Division One: Burnley had every reason to be pleased with their season's endeavours.

Before the start of the following season, the club announced that it was not to enter the Football League Cup, thereby effectively acknowledging a mistake made the previous season. Fixture congestion was to be even worse at the end of the 1961–62 season, and had the team had a good run in this competition, it is very difficult to see when these fixtures would have been played.

Burnley retained 38 players for the new season. The abolition of the maximum wage had little immediate effect. With average gates of almost 24,000, the club was able to offer the wage increases quickly and all the players re-signed. Bob Lord predicted in 1962 that 'the full effects of the abolition will not be seen for 3 or 4 years'.

The team that began the 1961–62 season (again against Arsenal) showed only one change from that which started the last (Harris for Pilkington). A good away point at Highbury was followed by home wins against Ipswich Town and Bolton Wanderers. The return match at Ipswich saw Alf Ramsey's newly-promoted team gain a convincing 6–2 victory, which launched their own Championship challenge.

Despite this setback, Burnley enjoyed a very profitable September with magnificent away wins at Birmingham City (6–2), Leicester City (6–2) and Fulham (5–3), which saw the Clarets four points clear at the top of the table by the end of the month. Centre forward, Ray Pointer was in prolific form, scoring nine goals in five games, including a hat-trick at Birmingham. September also saw an outburst of crowd trouble at Turf Moor. In a match against Everton, bottles were thrown onto the pitch. Police moved in, and removed some 16 Everton supporters from the Cricket Field End. The *Burnley Express* deplored what it called these 'South American-type antics'.

In December, Tommy Cummings succeeded Jimmy Hill as chairman of the PFA. It was a fitting tribute to Cummings, who had been out of the game for two seasons recently, but was now once again a regular member of the team. The 3–3 draw with Wolves on 18 November witnessed the first appearance of the new polo-necked shirts, whose first victory (4–2) was at Old Trafford the following week. Four goals were also put past both Sheffield clubs during December. By the turn of the year, Burnley were still top, but only by a point from Tottenham, who had won 4–2 in the clash between the two clubs at White Hart Lane back in October.

Leading the First Division, the Clarets went into 1962 with much optimism, which appeared to be justified – six goals in the FA Cup third round against QPR, six again the following week against Manchester City, seven against Birmingham City and when another six were put past West Ham in early March, Burnley had restored their four-point lead, and still had a game in hand over their nearest rivals, Ipswich Town.

Similar progress was being made in the FA Cup. A replay had been needed to dismiss Orient in the fourth round, Everton were beaten 3–1 in front of the largest Turf Moor crowd of the season (51,514), and Sheffield United were beaten 1–0 at Bramhall Lane, a week after the defeat of West Ham in the league. All looked set for Burnley to emulate Tottenham's double winning feat of the previous season.

The cup semi-final against Fulham was once again to be played at Villa Park, but any fears that Burnley may have had concerning that particular ground were dispelled by a league victory against Aston Villa the week before.

A superb display by Adam Blacklaw earned Burnley a 1–1 draw, and a replay at Filbert Street, Leicester, where two goals by Jimmy Robson put Burnley into the final against their great rivals, Tottenham Hotspur.

However, the Burnley team was beginning to feel the effects of a gruelling season, and a side lacking the steadying influence of McIlroy lost consecutive home matches to Manchester United (1–3) and Blackburn Rovers (0–1), and Ipswich went to the top of the league. McIlroy's return on Good Friday at home to Blackpool marked the first league win (2–0) for 4 weeks; Tommy Cummings' first goal since January 1952; and Burnley going back to first position – equal on points with Ipswich, but with a game in hand. The game in hand was wasted with a defeat at Sheffield United (who thus gained some revenge for their cup exit) and although a point was gained at

Blackpool on Easter Monday, Burnley found themselves two points behind Ipswich with just two games to play, but Burnley did have a superior goal average. If Burnley had won their last three games of the 1961–62 season, they would have won the double.

Already-relegated Chelsea came to Turf Moor with nothing to play for, and they were soon 1–0 down to a goal by Ian Towers, staking a claim for the left-wing position in the Cup Final team; Burnley were only 21 minutes away from maintaining their Championship challenge, when Tambling's shot deflected off Blunstone into the Burnley goal. Burnley had dropped a point, Ipswich had beaten Aston Villa and were Champions. A team including five reserves went down 4–0 at Sheffield Wednesday the following Monday, and all Burnley's hopes were switched to the FA Cup.

The only selection problem was at outside left, where Gordon Harris was preferred to Ian Towers, which left the team:

Blacklaw

Angus   Elder

Adamson   Cummings   Miller

Connelly   McIlroy   Pointer   Robson   Harris

This line-up had played together in 24 games, and had yet to be beaten.

Even after winning the double, the previous season, Spurs had had no hesitation in strengthening their squad by paying AC Milan £99,999 for the services of Jimmy Greaves. The two teams symbolised two completely different attitudes to success – home-produced Burnley against a Tottenham side that had cost over a quarter of a million pounds to put together.

Burnley were lifted during the week with the choice of Jimmy Adamson as the Football Writers' Footballer of the Year, but it was Tottenham's expensive signing, Greaves, who made the first impact at Wembley by scoring after just 3 minutes. Jimmy Robson equalised just after the interval, but this was cancelled out in the following minute by a Bobby Smith goal (despite the linesman flagging for a foul on Blacklaw). The game was sewn up for Spurs by an 82nd minute penalty by captain, Danny Blanchflower, after a handball by Tommy Cummings. It was Burnley's best display for weeks, but the cup stayed at Tottenham, where money had once again bought success, and Burnley ended up the season winning nothing.

Burnley's eventful, but ultimately unsuccessful, season produced an average home gate of 27,125 and this meant another profit for the club – of £23,375. Before the start of the new season, an effort was made to encourage families to come to Turf Moor, by reducing the price of season tickets for women. In the event, 8,070 tickets were sold making £34,233. The departure of Billy Marshall to Oldham left the club with 36 full-time professionals. The youth policy seemed to be working and new talents recently discovered included Willie Irvine (who scored a hat-trick on his reserve team debut), Willie Morgan, Arthur Bellamy, Brian O'Neil and Ralph Coates.

Burnley's second place in Division One brought the possibility of European football again to Turf Moor. The club, along with Everton, was nominated by the Football League for a place in the Inter-City Fairs Cup. Entry was not automatic however, and Burnley was refused entry as the town did not hold a fair.

The league campaign began disappointingly with a 3–1 home defeat by Everton. Jimmy Adamson missed the first 11 games of the season, which increased speculation as to his possible future in management. It was at this time that he turned down the chance of becoming England manager, and rumours of jobs at Peterborough and Ipswich came to nothing. At 33, he saw his immediate future as a player but his continued absence from the team disrupted the composition of the half back line.

Centre-half Cummings was replaced after only two games by John Talbut. At right half, Walter Joyce lost his place to David Walker, who had previously played only a handful of games in the 1960–61 season. The latter change took place after a disastrous 5–1 defeat by Birmingham City (Burnley had put 13 goals past them the previous season). This game also led to the introduction of Andy Lochhead into the forward line. Inside left Robson was dropped, and Lochhead came in at centre forward, displacing Pointer, who moved to inside right (where he had seldom played before), which meant McIlroy was switched to inside left.

The changes worked immediately – a home victory against Leyton Orient (2–0) started a ten game unbeaten run, including a 5–2 win at Old Trafford (with a John Connelly hat-trick) and a 5–1 victory over Sheffield United at Turf Moor. Lochhead scored ten goals in just nine games, and Burnley rose to second place. The run ended at Villa Park, but a 2–1 victory against Tottenham at Turf Moor put them back on course. When they met league leaders, Everton, in mid-December at Goodison Park, there were only two points separating the clubs. But within 24 minutes, Everton were three goals up, and a second-half goal by McIlroy saved only respectability.

The hard winter of 1962–63 was beginning to set in, and Burnley could only manage one more league game in the year. A dazzling display by Jimmy McIlroy inspired the Clarets to a 4–0 victory over Sheffield Wednesday, which took Burnley to one hundred goals for 1962 (in 50 games) and to third place in Division One.

The draw for the third round of the FA Cup produced a rematch of the 1961 semi-final and of the 1962 final, against Spurs. The match at White Hart Lane was twice postponed, and was finally played in the afternoon of Wednesday 16 January 1963. The afternoon kick-off (Tottenham feared a floodlight failure if the game were played at night) ensured that only a few hundred Burnley fans could make the trip. Ray Pointer was ruled out through injury, and he was replaced by Jimmy Robson (his first senior game since October), which made the Burnley team:

Blacklaw

Angus   Elder

Adamson   Talbut   Miller

Connelly   Robson   Lochhead   McIlroy   Harris

The game, watched by 32,756 spectators, was settled in the quarter hour either side of half time. Harris put Burnley into the lead 5 minutes before the interval, and goals by Connelly and Lochhead after the break sealed the victory. Tottenham had not lost an FA Cup tie since 1960 and refused to give in without a fight (on occasions literally, as both Dyson and Mackay, the skipper for the day, resorted to violence). Nevertheless, Burnley held on and the 3–0 victory marked, according to the *Burnley Express*, 'one of the club's best-ever achievements'.

1961–62 – Division One

Back: *Joyce, Elder, Cummings, Blacklaw, Miller, Angus, Harris*
Front: *Connelly, McIlroy, Pointer, Adamson, Robson, Towers*

Jimmy Adamson   *Jimmy McIlroy*

Jimmy Adamson and Jimmy McIlroy, two stalwarts of the early 1960s Burnley side. Adamson went on to become Chief Coach (1964–70) and Manager (1970–76), while McIlroy was transferred to Stoke City in 1963 in controversial circumstances. He now writes for the Burnley Express. *(Photographs © The Burnley Express)*

Chapter 2

Near the Top

(26 January 1963–18 April 1967)

By the start of 1963 the first effects of the abolition of the maximum wage were being felt. Burnley was well served by its youth policy, but on crowds of around 20,000, it was to prove increasingly difficult for the club to compete at the very top level. Star players would have to be sold but as long as they were adequately replaced, a very creditable playing standard could be maintained.

In the fourth round of the FA Cup, the Clarets were drawn at home to Liverpool, who were undefeated since Burnley had beaten them in early November. The first game, played on 26 January ended 1–1 – a John Connelly goal earned the replay at Anfield. Burnley were not involved in another competitive match until the return on 20 February. The cold weather may have deprived the team of match practice, but at least it allowed Pointer to regain fitness and he resumed at inside-right.

Elder put Burnley into the lead after 24 minutes, but Ian St John equalised on the stroke of half time. The game, played in front of a crowd of 57,906, went into extra-time. In the very last minute, Blacklaw's clearance struck St John, who was then brought down by the stranded Burnley keeper. From the ensuing penalty, Moran put Liverpool into the fifth round and also sparked off one of the most controversial incidents in Burnley FC's recent history.

The following Monday, Jimmy McIlroy was placed on the transfer list. On 5 March, only days before the transfer deadline, he went to Stoke City for around £25,000.

'The sale of Jimmy McIlroy . . . was a good piece of business,' claimed the chairman and on a purely financial basis, the club had done well to obtain so much for a 31-year old, but as an exercise in public relations, it was an unmitigated disaster. The local paper received only one letter in favour of the board's action, and over one hundred against. McIlroy was a great local celebrity and many people were offended by the treatment he received. Harry Potts' explanation ('he [McIlroy] would not give the effort and this is the reason – and the only reason – why he has left Burnley') was not widely believed, and the club lost some support because of its heavy-handedness.

McIlroy's initial successor was Jimmy Robson, who played the next four games at number ten without much success. He, in turn, was replaced by Arthur Bellamy, who made his debut in the 5–2 win at Manchester City on 26 March. Mike Buxton made his debut at left-back the following week, and with David Walker also in the side, the average age was only 22. A 4–0 home win over Fulham on Good Friday put Burnley six points behind leaders, Leicester City, with two games in hand, but any hopes of a late Championship bid were dashed by a 7–2 defeat at Wolves the following day.

The benefits of the youth policy showed in an increasing number of young players coming through the ranks. Willie Morgan, Brian O'Neil and Willie Irvine all made their debuts before the end of the season, whilst Tommy Cummings, at the club since 1948, accepted the manager's job at Mansfield Town. Peter Simpson and Ian Towers were both tried at inside-left, but McIlroy's successor was discovered only in the penultimate game of the season at Arsenal. An injury to Towers necessitated a switch inside for Gordon Harris, who proved a revelation in the position and retained it for most of the remainder of his time at Burnley. In the same game, Irvine marked his debut with a goal, and a hat-trick in the last game at home to Birmingham City promised great things for the future. Despite the changes, the team still managed to finish third in the league.

Average gates of 25,180 left the club in a healthy enough position to refuse an offer of £23,000 from Stoke City for Ian Towers. Towers had asked for a transfer because he was paid a varying wage, dependent on whether he played for the first-team or reserves, and he was asking for parity with the regular first-teamers. Nevertheless the only major close season departure from Turf Moor was Peter Simpson, who was given a free transfer to Bury following his appearance in a local court case.

Burnley started the 1963–64 season without Alex Elder, who broke an ankle in pre-season training. The first victory came in the third game at home to Sheffield Wednesday, with the team:

Blacklaw

Angus   Joyce

Walker   Talbut   Miller

Morgan   Robson   Pointer   Harris   Connelly

In the early part of the season, the team varied considerably. No fewer than 22 players were injured in the first 3 months, but nonetheless some good results were achieved: an Arthur Bellamy hat-trick helped inflict Everton's first home league defeat in 43 matches; and two wins over Blackburn put Burnley into fourth place in mid-October. Injuries meant debuts for diminutive winger, Johnny Price at West Ham, and for full-back, Freddie Smith at Stoke, where Burnley came from 3–0 down to draw 4–4. A win at home to Ipswich in December put Burnley only four points behind leaders, Leeds United, but a more telling statistic was the attendance – a post-war league low of 10,358.

Elder returned to the team just before Christmas, and on Boxing Day, Andy Lochhead scored four in a 6–1 defeat of Manchester United in front of a much better crowd of 35,764. (This victory was avenged 2 days later at Old Trafford when United won 5–1.)

With Harris and Connelly restored to the team after injury, Burnley progressed to the sixth round of the FA Cup by defeating Rotherham (after a replay), Newport County and Huddersfield Town. Despite a fine performance, they went down 3–2 to the eventual winners, West Ham United.

During early 1964, the Clarets slipped into the bottom half of the league, where they had not finished since the 1951–52 season. Nevertheless, the club continued to sell players. In February, Walter Joyce, the reserve team captain, went to Blackburn for £13,000; Trevor Meredith was later sold to Shrewsbury Town for a small fee; and more seriously in April, John Connelly went to Manchester United for a sum in excess of £40,000. Earlier in the season, after two of his goals had helped Burnley to a 3–2 win over West Bromwich Albion, the *Burnley Express* had proclaimed: 'They must not make the mistake of parting company AT ANY PRICE with John Connelly.'

However, Ian Towers replaced him at outside left for the final two games of the season. Towers scored twice in a 3–1 win at Notts Forest and in the last game at home to Spurs, the Clarets, with

Sammy Todd making his debut at right-back, ran out 7–2 winners. Burnley finished ninth and the seven goals (two each for Harris, O'Neil and Irvine, one for Lochhead) silenced much of the justifiable criticism of the sale of Connelly.

For only the third time since the war, the club reported a financial loss on the year up to March 1964. The figure of £7,881 was amply compensated for by the money made on Connelly. One of the major items of expenditure was wages, which amounted to £99,057 (from £81,317 the previous year). This was still not enough for Alex Elder, who demanded a pay rise and to be put on the transfer list. 'I would like to get to a city club, where the rewards are higher all round,' he told one reporter. His demands were refused, and he took his case to the Football League.

Financial pressures led the board to suspend its plans to build a new stand, and sensibly transfer monetary priorities to the playing side. Elder stayed at the club, and was in the team for the opening game of the 1964–65 season at home to Blackpool:

Blacklaw

Angus   Elder

O'Neil   Talbut   Miller

Morgan   Lochhead   Irvine   Harris   Towers

Elder was injured in the 2–2 draw, and Burnley were without a win for eight matches, until a 3–2 defeat of West Ham on 19 September. Jimmy Adamson announced that he was to retire at the end of the season and was promptly appointed as chief coach. Elder signed a full contract at the end of the month, but bad results continued and – after a 0–0 home draw with Manchester United – Burnley found themselves in 18th position.

John Angus' first two goals for the club could not prevent defeat at Highbury and another setback at home to Leeds sent Burnley further down the table. Pointer and Robson were scoring heavily in the reserves, and both were brought in to lead the attack, but without success. A 5–1 home defeat by Liverpool led to wholesale changes (there had already been 53 team changes that season). In the next match, at Blackpool on 12 December, a 4–2–4 system was adopted:

Blacklaw

Smith   Miller   Todd   Elder

O'Neil   Harris

Towers   Lochhead   Irvine   Price

The new 'Double Spearhead' of Lochhead and Irvine got all four goals (Lochhead a hat-trick) and Burnley reeled off four straight victories in which Irvine scored seven. The second of these wins against Sheffield United marked the debut of Ralph Coates, a young forward from Hetton-le-Hole, birthplace of Harry Potts.

In the new year (1965), Willie Morgan, who had been dropped, was 'fined and disciplined' for a breach of training regulations. The run of league wins was ended at Everton, but steady progress was being made in the FA Cup. Replays were needed to dismiss Brentford and Reading, and Burnley were drawn to meet Manchester United in the fifth round. In the league match between the teams the week before the cup-tie, Les Latcham made his debut at outside left. Burnley went down 3–2, but were without the services of Lochhead. He was recalled for the cup match and put the Clarets into the lead after 16 minutes. The score remained the same until the 85th minute when George Best, who had just lost a boot, crossed for Denis Law to equalise. Best had not time to put his boot back on, when his stockinged foot laid on the winner for Paddy Crerand.

League form, however, was improving, and two goals by Irvine helped to defeat Blackburn Rovers 4–1 at Ewood Park in February. The success of the 'Double Spearhead' meant that Burnley could allow Jimmy Robson to go to Blackpool for around £10,000. After a 5–1 defeat at Leeds, Adam Blacklaw picked up an injury in training, and was replaced by the young Scot, Harry Thomson. Thomson saved a penalty in his debut at Leicester, where Burnley ran out 2–0 winners – one of the goals came from Coates, now playing at outside left, and about to establish himself as the eventual successor to John Connelly in that position. Such was the improvement, that both Potts and Adamson were offered new 5-year contracts with substantial pay increases, which made Adamson the highest paid coach in football. This showed great faith in the coaching staff, based on the well-founded belief that another very good side had been created and was ready to challenge for honours.

The need for success was shown by the declining gates at the end of the season, where, once the threat of relegation had receded (around Christmas), the team had little to play for. Only 10,106, another post-war low, turned up to watch the home draw against Aston Villa. The return of Jimmy McIlroy merited a slightly bigger crowd, and they saw a Willie Irvine goal (put past his brother Bobby, the Stoke goalkeeper) give Burnley victory. As in the previous season, the last game gave much scope for confidence. Andy Lochhead scored five, as Burnley beat a weakened Chelsea team, 6–2. Tommy Docherty, the Chelsea manager, had dropped seven first team members on disciplinary charges, but nonetheless, Burnley's performance, with Dave Merrington making his debut in defence, gave cause for satisfaction. Lochhead's goalscoring feat made him only the fourth player to score five or more goals in a match (only Jimmy Robson had done it since the war) and it earned Burnley 12th place in the league. They had won as many games as they had lost (16) and scored as many goals as they had conceded (70).

Undoubtedly, they had improved in the latter part of the season, and it was therefore possible to sell some of the reserve strength. David Walker went to Southampton for a fee in excess of £10,000; Johnny Price went to Stockport County for £4,000; and in August, Ray Pointer was transferred to Bury for around £7,000. These transactions did not seriously affect the first-team playing strength and did bring in some much-needed cash.

Before the start of the 1965–66 season, Alex Elder was appointed club captain, and the side made a confident start. After four games (including two 3–1 victories over Blackpool), Burnley were top of the league. The team at Blackpool read:

Thomson

Angus   Talbut   Miller   Elder

O'Neil   Harris

Morgan   Lochhead   Irvine   Coates

This was the first season that substitutes were permitted in the Football League and Ian Towers earned the distinction of being the first Burnley substitute to be called upon, when he replaced Willie Irvine at Liverpool. The first defeat of the season came at Everton on 4 September, but an Irvine hat-trick 3 days later helped to beat Northampton Town (4–1) and further victories over Manchester United (3–0) and Northampton again (2–1) kept Burnley at the top. A 4–1 defeat at home to Blackburn knocked the team off its stride, but by mid-November, after a tremendous 4–0 victory at Sunderland (including two goals by Coates), Burnley were back in first position.

They had also reached the last eight of the Football League Cup, and were favourites to win it. It was the first time that they had entered the competition since reaching the semi-finals in 1961, and victories over Doncaster, Southampton and Stoke put them into the quarter-finals. The visit to Third Division Peterborough United proved to be a disaster, as the First Division leaders crashed to a 4–0 defeat.

Blacklaw had re-established himself in the team, after Thomson was suspended for a breach of training regulations (as was Lochhead). His recall prompted him to withdraw an earlier transfer request. Dave Merrington had also won a regular place in the middle of defence alongside the ever-present, Brian Miller.

Burnley had already been overtaken by Liverpool when the two teams met at Anfield on 27 November and a 2–1 Liverpool win extended their lead at the top. The Clarets kept hard on their heels with a good win at Fulham (5–2, including an Irvine hat-trick) and a 4–2 win against Leicester City. Irvine failed to score in the Leicester game and therefore only equalled Ray Pointer's club record of scoring in seven consecutive league matches.

On New Year's Day 1966, Willie Morgan became only the fifth Burnley player ever to be sent off. He was dismissed in a stormy match at Blackburn for aiming a flying kick at Rovers' centre-half, Mike England. Burnley still won 2–0 and remained second, two points behind Liverpool with a game in hand. Andy Lochhead again scored five in one match – in the FA Cup third round replay against Bournemouth (7–0). But cup hopes were dashed in the next round at White Hart Lane, where Alan Gilzean's 88th minute goal gave Spurs victory by the odd goal in seven.

Blacklaw was rested after the cup defeat, but missed only two games as Thomson was forced to drop out with a broken hand. Merrington, too, lost his place in the team. In March, the young Irishman, Sammy Todd, became Miller's regular partner. One departure from Turf Moor was that of Ian Towers. He had started only one match all season (in the League Cup at Doncaster) and was transferred to Oldham Athletic in January for 'a sizeable fee'. He had been deprived of a first-team place by the consistency of Coates and Harris – Harris was selected to play for England in January, but made a disappointing debut against Poland.

Liverpool came to Turf Moor on 23 April, already in the European Cup Winners' Cup Final and needing only a point to clinch the Championship. They did not get it, as goals by Irvine and Coates gave Burnley victory in front of a crowd of 36,741. It was Irvine's 29th league goal of the season (a post-war Burnley record) and his 41st in all competitions. The last home game of the season witnessed a bizarre own goal from Alex Elder for Leeds United, which helped the Yorkshire club clinch second place on goal average. Burnley thus finished third in the 1965–66 season, even though they had an identical playing record to the Championship-winning side of 1959–60. Like then, Burnley qualified for European competition – entrance into the Fairs Cup was now virtually automatic, dependent only on league position. It had been a good season for Harry Potts' young side, and he called it 'a grand augury for the future'. The *Burnley Express* agreed: 'Providing Burnley can keep most of this team together, they can keep the club at the top for years to come.'

As if to emphasise this seemingly bright future, the club entered a team in an under–21 tournament in Dusseldorf. In the group, the Burnley side defeated Fortuna Dusseldorf, FC Cologne and Inter Milan. They thus qualified for the final, where goals by Coates and Gary France gave them a 2–1 victory over Barcelona. Coates was named Player of the Tournament, and he scored a further two goals to earn his team a draw against a German Select Youth XI.

Despite the success of the season, the club announced a profit of only £1,966, which included £43,120 made on transfers. For the first time, the wage bill topped £100,000. The somewhat precarious financial position did not stop the club unveiling new plans for a new social and recreational centre to be built under a new seated stand at the Bee Hole End. Some optimism had been created by the weekly draw raffle of the Turf Moor Development Association, launched in October 1965. Plans were also announced to start half-time bingo from September. The belief that such fundraising could provide the cash for ground redevelopment **as well** as keeping the potentially-successful side together was to prove naive and futile.

The new season (1966–67) started even better than the previous one. A hat-trick from Gordon 'Bomber' Harris in the first game set up a 4–0 victory over Sheffield United; Len Kinsella made his debut in place of the injured Ralph Coates in another home win against Fulham (3–0); and Brian O'Neil got both goals in a 2–1 win at West Brom. The first point dropped was in a goalless draw at Fulham, and another was lost when Alex Elder missed a penalty at home to Leeds United. The Leeds game again proved a rough one, with five bookings – in games between the clubs during the previous two seasons, the referee had twice had to deliver a lecture to the 22 players in order to cool the situation. Another draw, at Everton, took Burnley to the top of Division One.

As leaders, Burnley re-entered Europe. They were originally drawn to play Hanover, but after protests from VFP Stuttgart, who finished above Hanover in the league, the Clarets travelled to Stuttgart. It was decided to play the first leg of the Fairs Cup tie in Germany, so as not to clash with the following week's beer festival and a crowd of 10,000 saw a Willie Irvine goal earn Burnley's seventh consecutive draw. Towards the end, Brian O'Neil was sent off and consequently had to miss the second leg. In the return, goals by Lochhead and Coates gave Burnley an easy victory.

Despite Bob Lord's wish that 'the day will never come when Burnley has to buy a player', the club announced an interest in John Connelly. A bid of £40,000 for the unsettled ex-Claret increased speculation as to the future of Willie Morgan. Tommy Docherty, the Chelsea manager, had travelled to Stuttgart to watch him, and reputedly offered £70,000 for the Scottish winger. But because of Lord's aversion to signing-on fees, Connelly chose Blackburn Rovers, and Morgan remained a Burnley player.

In October, Ralph Coates was selected for the England under–23 squad. This made eleven internationals at Burnley – seven full (Blacklaw, Angus, Elder, Todd, Miller, Irvine and Harris) and four at under–23 level (Talbut, O'Neil, Lochhead and Coates). Burnley continued well in the league – a 3–1 win at Chelsea was achieved with Bellamy (wearing the number nine shirt) acting as sweeper. Irvine was restored the following week to a side which defeated Leicester City 5–2, and put Burnley into third place, just two points behind the leaders, Spurs.

During the previous few years, there had been a notable upsurge in crowd violence, and in October, the standing areas behind both goals were railed off. The throwing of missiles had become an increasing problem – at one match in the previous season, the police had found on the pitch, fifty steel washers, four small batteries and a sharply-pointed can opener. Police mingling with the crowd had little effect and the Burnley chief constable was fighting a losing battle, when he announced, 'We have **got** to cut this trouble out, before it gets too late'. In one national newspaper, the Burnley fans were placed fourth in an obscene language chanting league, and sporadic disturbances were too numerous to catalogue.

In the next round of the Fairs Cup, Burnley were drawn against the Swiss team, Lausanne Sports. In Lausanne, Bellamy was again played in a defensive role, and despite going behind, Burnley ran out 3–1 winners through headed goals by Coates, Harris and Lochhead. Coates sustained an injury in this match and missed the return. O'Neil was switched to outside left and Irvine resumed in attack. The changes worked – both O'Neil and Irvine got a goal and Andy Lochhead's hat-trick sealed an impressive victory.

The injury to Coates meant a league debut for John Murray at Leicester in November, and the same week Gary France came on as substitute when Arthur Bellamy broke his leg at Liverpool. Against Aston Villa, Lochhead got all four goals in a victory which kept Burnley in the top six. Two Christmas defeats by Stoke City led to Blacklaw once again being dropped, and Thomson took his place against West Bromwich Albion on 31 December. Making his debut for Albion was John Talbut, who had been unable to gain a regular spot in the Burnley team because of the consistency of Miller and Todd. His transfer earned £32,000 for Burnley and after only 4 minutes of the game, he scored his first, and only, goal for the Turf Moor club, when he headed into his own net, and Burnley went on to win 5–1.

Just before the third round Fairs Cup tie with Naples, Alex Elder was injured in a game at Newcastle. Substitute, Les Latcham got his first opportunity to play at left back, but it was Freddie Smith who deputised for Elder against the Italians. When the draw had been made in December, the Naples coach, Enrico Zuppardi, had said, 'Harris, Lochhead, Irvine and Turf Moor are all new names to us, though I am sure they are all first-rate players.' But there can be little doubt that Naples did underestimate Burnley, as they came without four of their star players. Omar Sivori, European Footballer of the Year in 1961, had pulled a muscle in training, but the others, Bianchi and Juliano (both internationals), and club captain, Pierluigi Ronson, were merely rested. Goals from Coates, Latcham and Lochhead gave

Burnley a 3–0 first leg lead, against a ten-man Naples team, who had Panzanato sent off in the 35th minute for kicking Lochhead.

The return in Naples on 8 February, watched by a crowd of 60,000, was marked by a tremendous performance by Harry Thomson, including a penalty save from Altafini. A magnificent defensive display, with only Morgan, Lochhead and Coates upfield, and Latcham shadowing Sivori, earned a 0–0 draw and a quarter final tie with Eintracht Frankfurt.

In the 1967 FA Cup, Burnley were drawn against the holders, Everton. The first game at Turf Moor resulted in a goalless draw. In the replay, Everton took the lead through Alex Young, and Willie Irvine equalised for the Clarets. But in a 58th minute clash with Everton's Morrisey, Irvine broke his leg and had to be stretchered off. Everton went on to win 2–1 and Burnley's trophy hopes lay solely with the Fairs Cup.

The injury to Irvine proved costly, as no real replacement was found to lead the attack. Colin Blant (born in nearby Rawtenstall) was tried and did score a couple of goals at Blackpool in only his second game, but his inexperience meant that he was not risked in the European games. (In the same game, at Blackpool, Thomson saved another penalty and had now saved all three he had faced for Burnley.) League form was suffering and three defeats at Easter put them in the bottom half of the table. A morale-boosting 2–0 win over Sheffield Wednesday on 1 April was tempered by the loss of Andy Lochhead for the Fairs Cup tie.

The absence of both central strikers was not felt too much in the first leg in Frankfurt, where a Brian Miller goal earned a draw, but back at Turf Moor, a blunt 'double spearhead' of Les Latcham and Brian O'Neil proved ineffective. A late Miller goal was Burnley's only consolation in a demoralising 2–1 defeat.

So Burnley were out of Europe (for good, as it turned out). But in April 1967, the prospects still looked good. What was still a young team had been deprived of further European glory by injuries to key players, but if this squad could be kept together, then it appeared that it could still achieve much and had surely not yet reached its height.

In February 1967, Burnley Football Club bought a strip of land from the adjoining cricket club. The plans for ground-development at the Bee Hole End were switched to this new site. Four years previously, Bob Lord had doubted whether Burnley could retain its

First Division status 'for the simple reason we shall just not be able to compete.' In spite of the precarious financial position, the board twice refused to register the transfer of shares of Luther Wilkinson. Eric Cookson, a local businessman, and Ken Bates, the future Chelsea chairman, both tried to buy his shares, but both offers were turned down by the board – thus possible investors in the club's future were missed.

Nonetheless, Burnley had maintained its position amongst the top clubs in the country. This had been achieved in the face of financial pressures from outside; but the grandiose redevelopment plans were to prove a self-inflicted injury.

1967–68 – Division One

Back: O'Neil, Thomson, Bellamy
Middle: Morgan, Casper, Irvine, Latcham, Ternent(R), Coates
Front: Angus, Lochhead, Waldron

Bob Lord, butcher and Burnley chairman. The dominant figure at the club throughout the 1960s and 1970s. (Photograph © The Burnley Express)

Chapter 3

The Fourteenth Best Team In England

(April 1967-May 1970)

The period up to 1970 was to prove another time of rebuilding, and the process started almost immediately. In the same week as the Eintracht game, the club signed Michael Docherty, 16-year-old son of Tommy. Docherty senior praised Burnley as the finest soccer academy in the country. A sound judgement, as his son went on to play for England Youth and also to captain Burnley's triumphant Youth Cup side of 1968. This team was to form the basis of Burnley's immediate plans, as the side that had reached the Fairs Cup quarter-finals was dismantled.

The first to depart were Alex Elder and Brian Miller. With only four matches remaining of the 1966–67 season, Elder was suspended for a breach of club regulations and he resigned the captaincy. In the first game after the European defeat, at Villa Park, Miller suffered the knee injury which ended his playing career (although he did remain at the club as part of the coaching staff).

The season ended disappointingly with a 4–1 home defeat by Arsenal, and, despite the return of Elder, a 7–0 thrashing at Hillsborough (Harry Thomson once again saved a penalty). The last match at home to Everton saw the debut of Dave Thomas. At 16 years 220 days, he was the youngest Burnley player to appear in Division One (Tommy Lawton was younger when he made his debut in 1936 in Division Two). The game ended in a 1–1 draw and Burnley finished the season in 14th position.

The obviously unsettled Elder was placed on the transfer list, as was Adam Blacklaw. Blacklaw was transferred to Blackburn Rovers in July for £15,000 and the Elder deal brought in a further £50,000 from Stoke City. The club announced a net loss of £1,543 and a wage bill of £116,241. The average attendance was up at 20,507 and Burnley decided to break with tradition and buy a player. Striker Frank Casper was purchased from Rotherham United for £27,000. 'What we cannot afford to do is to go into the Second Division,' said Bob Lord, 'if we stuck to our earlier aim not to buy, we would deserve to be called arrogant fools.'

The acquisition of Martin Dobson, a young centre forward released by Bolton Wanderers, brought the playing strength up to 31. The new season (1967–68) began with a 2–1 home win against Coventry (a debut goal for Casper and one for Irvine). The same scorers could not prevent a 4–2 defeat at West Ham. Three more goals earned only a point in the return at Turf Moor, but 4 days later, five goals were enough to end Tottenham's 33-match unbeaten run. Gordon Harris, the new club captain, had been moved back in an attempt to shore up the suspect defence which left the team:

Thomson

Smith   Angus   Harris   Latcham

O'Neil   Bellamy

Morgan   Casper   Lochhead   Coates

The defence, however, continued to let in goals. A 2–0 lead with 5 minutes left was surrendered at Old Trafford, and a 3–2 defeat at Wolverhampton meant that although Burnley were top scorers in the league, they were only in 12th position. Worse was to follow in November at West Bromwich Albion, where the Clarets went down to an 8–1 defeat (a late goal by Bellamy ensured that Burnley had still scored in every game). Centre half, Colin Waldron had been signed from Chelsea for £30,000 in October, but made little impression in his first season. For a League Cup match at Arsenal, Andy Lochhead played in a sweeper's role, but this could not prevent elimination from the tournament (1–2).

A 5–1 defeat at Coventry in December, which put Burnley into fourteenth position, followed the club's suspension of Gordon Harris on a disciplinary matter. It was alleged that he had been seen having a night out just prior to the Arsenal cup tie. Like Elder 6 months previously, Harris was unhappy at the club. His wife claimed that he was being made the scapegoat for the team's poor form and in January 1968 he moved to Sunderland for £70,000. The mood of the club filtered down even to the mascot, Paul Lonsdale, who quit his post after being 'cold-shouldered' at the pre-match kick-ins. Another more senior departure was that of Willie Irvine. He had lost his first-team place around the turn of the year, and despite his admirable scoring rate of 78 goals in 123 appearances, he was allowed to go to Preston North End for £45,000.

In the new year (1968) demolition work began on the old Cricket Field Stand, and with new facilities the emphasis was placed on youth in the team. 18-year-old Ray Ternent came in for his first game at full-back in December (Ray was no relation to Stan Ternent who played a handful of games at centre half during 1967). Rod Jones, the young goalkeeper signed from Rotherham, made an unhappy debut in the 4–3 defeat at Fulham.

In the FA Youth Cup, Steve Kindon made an impressive start with two goals in the 4–3 win over Manchester City. Further victories over Manchester United, Sheffield United and Everton put the team into a two-legged final against Coventry City. Much attention was paid to the exploits of the youth team as the senior squad's season ended with no cause for excitement. Defeat at Arsenal was the 16th loss in 21 away games (the worst away record in the league), but Burnley's home form was sufficiently good for them to again claim 14th position with a last-game 3–0 win over Leeds United.

The youth team went down 2–1 in the first leg at Coventry. In the return at Turf Moor (10 May), Coventry goalkeeper David Icke, the future broadcaster and conservationist, was stunned in a first half collision, and did not reappear for the second period. Burnley took full advantage and two goals by local-born David Hartley clinched the trophy for the young team of:

McEvoy

Jones   Docherty   Wrigley   Cliff

Probert   West

Hartley   Brown   Thomas   Kindon

In the mind of Jimmy Adamson, this success was the single most important event during his coaching career and he was determined to build on it. Of the eleven, only Gerry McEvoy and David Hartley did not reach the first team, and the Youth Cup victory cannot be underestimated in its influence on Adamson's future plans.

During the close season, the club was described in a government report as 'a phenomenon perhaps explicable only in terms of superb management'. More of the same was required to deal with the increase in wages. The bill for the previous year amounted to £123,263 and several players had to be released. Stan Ternent went to Carlisle United for £4,000, Gary France to Bury and Mick Buxton to Halifax (Buxton had made over 300 reserve team appearances, but fewer than 20 for the first team). The biggest loss, however, occurred when Willie Morgan refused to re-sign for the club. Nevertheless, there was a ready-made replacement in Dave Thomas, and he took his place in the team which drew at Nottingham Forest (2–2, with two goals in the last 10 minutes from Waldron and Casper):

Thomson

Angus   Waldron   Merrington   Latcham

O'Neil   Bellamy

Coates   Lochhead   Casper   Thomas

Three days later, Peter Jones made his debut and by the end of the month, two of his youth team colleagues had done likewise. Willie Brown made his only Burnley appearance, coming on as substitute at West Bromwich Albion (2–3), and Steve Kindon played in the 5–0 defeat at West Ham. Away form went from bad to worse with a 7–0 loss at Tottenham, and moves were made to strengthen the squad. The sale of Morgan to Manchester United brought in £117,000 which allowed the club to purchase Jim Thomson from Chelsea for a club record of £40,000. Thomson's debut on 5 October brought no improvement, as his new team went down 4–0 to Liverpool. This defeat prompted wholesale changes for the forthcoming match at West Ham:

Thomson

Smith   Waldron   Blant   Latcham

Coates   Dobson

Thomas   Murray   Casper   Kindon

Colin Waldron captained the side, which had an average age of 22, and goals by John Murray, Steve Kindon and Martin Dobson gave the Clarets a 3–1 victory, which sparked off an eight-game winning sequence, most notably a 5–1 thrashing of that season's Champions, Leeds United. The form of John Murray (eight goals in eight games) earned him a call-up to the England under–23 squad, and also caused the club to accept Leicester City's offer of £70,000 for Andy Lochhead. A product of the youth policy, Lochhead had scored over 100 league goals for Burnley, but at the age of 27 he was deemed dispensable from a team so heavily dependent on youth. Both parts of the once-feared 'Double Spearhead' of Irvine and Lochhead had now left Turf Moor. Obviously, such money could only be obtained from the sale of *experienced* players, but as a leader of the attack, Lochhead was not adequately replaced.

The winning run was ended in a home draw with Wolves, but victories over Leicester City and Crystal Palace had secured a League Cup semi-final tie with Swindon Town. In the first leg, Peter Noble, making his first visit to Turf Moor, scored the winner for the Third Division team. The 2–1 scoreline was reversed in the second leg and a decider was played at the ground of West Bromwich Albion. Swindon took an early lead, which Dave Thomas equalised in the last minute to send the game into extra time. Frank Casper scored only a minute after the restart, but an own goal by Arthur Bellamy and another Noble effort robbed Burnley of a place in the final.

In the league, away form continued badly. Fourteen defeats on their travels ensured Burnley once again took 14th place. Attendances were the lowest in Division One (eight Division Two averages were higher, as was Swindon's in Division Three). Despite this fall in revenue, the club announced plans to build a £400,000 entertainment centre on the Brunshaw Road site. The complex would contain a club room, a restaurant, a theatre, a shop and a cafeteria. A 300-yard frontage on Brunshaw Road was envisaged, incorporating the new stand. The chairman wanted a ground fit for the success which was promised by an improving young team.

Steve Kindon had established himself as a regular member of the first-team squad, and there were debuts during November and December for Eric Probert, Wilf Wrigley and Michael Docherty. Kindon, Docherty and Dave Thomas were all members of the England youth squad, and their fortunes contrasted with those of John Murray. Although a member of the England under–23 squad earlier in the season, he was unable to get back into the first team at Burnley after an injury in November. Four months later, he asked to be put on the transfer list, where he was joined by two experienced, but unsettled, players Brian O'Neil and Sammy Todd. By the start of the following season, however, both O'Neil and Todd had settled their differences with the club (although only for one more year). The only senior departure of the 1969 close season was that of Harry Thomson. He became another victim of the strict disciplinary regulations at Turf Moor. In May, he was actually sacked by the club, and initially signed with non-league Bacup Borough before joining Blackpool in July.

For a goalkeeping replacement, Burnley turned to Peter Mellor. Previously on a month's trial from Cheshire League, Witton Albion, he was now signed on a permanent basis for £2,000. He made a magnificent debut in the goalless draw at Derby, despite dislocating a finger.

The new Cricket Field Stand was opened before the start of the season (1969–70). In the first home game, Burnley displayed their new shirts of claret with blue trimmings. A 3–3–4 formation was tried:

Mellor

Latcham   Waldron   Todd

O'Neil   Probert   Docherty

Thomas   Kindon   Casper   Coates

The substitute was Geoff Nulty, who had been acquired on a free transfer the previous season after being released by Stoke City. A goal by Kindon and two by Casper (who also missed a penalty) were enough to beat Sunderland. This was Burnley's only win in the opening thirteen league games, largely due to a failure to score further goals. A defeat at West Ham in early October left them in twentieth place but another victory over Sunderland (1–0) and two 4–2 wins against Crystal Palace and Sheffield Wednesday respectively restored some respectability to league position.

Michael Docherty, only 19, captained the side against Everton in November, but lost this role to Dave Merrington, who was appointed club captain just before Christmas. Many of the older players were feeling unsettled – Colin Blant, Len Kinsella and Doug Collins all joined John Murray on the transfer list. A £45,000 move to Newcastle United for Collins fell through at the last minute, and in March, Murray finally left the club to go to Blackpool for £10,000. The ground was changing along with the team, and most of the season was played in front of three sides of spectators, as the old Brunshaw Road Stand was demolished.

David Wilson, who had been signed from Walsall in September for £12,000, made his first full appearance in the FA Cup victory (3–0) over Wolves at Turf Moor. In the following round, Burnley were drawn away at Chelsea, where two goals by Martin Dobson in the last 10 minutes secured a replay. Dobson was now playing regularly in the middle of defence, but he was switched forward in a shrewd tactical move by Merrington. In the replay, it was Chelsea's turn to come from behind, and they won 3–1 after extra time.

League form seemed to be improving, and the promise of so many youngsters augured well for the future. Kindon hit the first Burnley hat-trick since Lochhead's last in 1966, in a 5–0 thrashing of Nottingham Forest at Turf Moor on 21 February 1970. This game proved to be Harry Potts' final one in charge of the team. The following Monday, Jimmy Adamson was named as the new manager and Potts became general manager. The move stemmed from the desire to retain Adamson's services. His contract as coach ran out in April, and his name had already been linked with other managerial positions. The new appointment succeeded in keeping him at Turf Moor for a further 6 years.

It was clear that Adamson's aspirations lay with the younger players and an experimental team was announced for the game against Stoke City on Good Friday:

Mellor (22 years old)

Docherty (19)   Wrigley (20)   Dobson (22)   Ternent (21)

West (18)   Coates (23)   Probert (18)

Thomas (18)   Nulty (21)   Kindon (19)

Probert scored after only 3 minutes to give Burnley a lead which they held for 82 minutes before Stoke's equaliser. Six of the team (Docherty, Wrigley, West, Probert, Thomas and Kindon) had played in the 1968 Youth Cup team; three (Mellor, Dobson and Thomas) were members of the England under–23 squad; and one (Ralph Coates) had just been named in Alf Ramsey's party of 28 for the Mexico World Cup.

Only one defeat in the last eight games yet again placed Burnley in 14th position, but there was great optimism that next season's position would be much higher, and that Burnley would soon once again become a major footballing force. 'We have the youngest group of experienced players in the First Division,' said Adamson, 'and possibly the largest group of experienced players. What I want now is the youngest, largest and **best** group of experienced players.'

Some of the senior professionals were sold: Freddie Smith and Colin Blant went to Portsmouth for a combined sum of £15,000; Sammy Todd went to Sheffield Wednesday for £40,000; and Brian O'Neil to Southampton for £75,000. The sale of O'Neil, which came as no great surprise, meant that of the 13 players selected for the first two rounds of the Fairs Cup three seasons previously only three (Angus, Bellamy and Latcham) remained on the playing staff. Around £400,000 had been collected for this side, only a quarter of which had been spent on new players.

One new stand had been built, another was in the planning stages, but seemingly the most impressive rebuilding had taken place on the field of play, where a team based around Ralph Coates, Martin Dobson, Peter Mellor and the 1968 youth team appeared capable of more than holding its own in the First Division. The illusion was to last only one season.

Chapter 4

'The Team of the Seventies'

(May 1970–10 June 1975)

'Burnley will be the team of the seventies. We are building one of the finest stadiums in the country and we have a great young team to go with it. In the next few years we will win the Championship not once but several times. Everything looks good and we are ready to go. Ability of this calibre has just got to break through.'

So spoke Jimmy Adamson at a pre-season press conference. Such was his confidence that he had recommended seven of his squad for the England under–23 team, when asked by Alf Ramsey. There was a new first team trainer, Brian Miller. He had been promoted in July in succession to George Bray, who took over Miller's position as reserve team coach. The new season also saw the launch of the match programme, *The Claret and Blue*, and Jack Butterfield, the Commercial Manager, announced the opening of 14 refreshment bars (eight licensed) inside the ground. In the general air of optimism, Adamson struck a note of caution, when he admitted that it was 'the hardest start I can ever remember'.

Preparations went badly. Martin Dobson broke his leg in a pre-season game at Middlesbrough; Peter Mellor dislocated his left shoulder in training; and Peter Jones also suffered a broken leg. In the close season, Adamson had attended a football management course at Loughborough University. Also on the course was Tony Waiters, then a coach at Liverpool. Waiters had retired from playing in June 1967, but was persuaded to return with Burnley. A fee of £2,000 was paid to Blackpool, his last club, and owing to Mellor's injury, Waiters played in the opening game at home to Liverpool. An edgy performance ended in a 2–1 defeat. The first point of the season came from a 1–1 draw with Champions, Everton, with the team:

Waiters

Angus   Waldron   Thomson   Merrington

Bellamy   Docherty   Coates

Thomas   Probert   Kindon

Another draw was earned at Manchester City (holders of the European Cup Winners' Cup), but a home defeat by Manchester United made it the worst start since 1964. It got worse.

A 3–0 defeat by Leeds United was followed by a goalless draw with the previous year's other FA Cup finalists, Chelsea. Even a clash with bottom club, Ipswich Town meant a 3–0 defeat and sent Burnley to the foot of the league.

As Bob Lord was a member of the Football League Management Committee the draw for the third round of the League Cup was held at Turf Moor in September. Unfortunately, the home team was not in it, having suffered a 2–0 defeat at the hands of Third Division Aston Villa, who included Andy Lochhead in their line-up.

An own goal in the 2–1 loss at Arsenal was Burnley's first score for seven games. Three goals did come in the home leg of the Texaco Cup tie with Hearts, but at the cost of an ankle injury to Steve Kindon. In the second leg an out-of-touch Waiters conceded four and Burnley went out of the competition. Dave Thomas became the first Burnley scorer in the league for 763 minutes. Waldron also scored in the same game, but defensive errors gave Wolves a 3–2 win. Five successive defeats were halted by a goalless draw with Coventry City, but a 2–0 defeat at Liverpool meant only four points from 13 games, and the club four points adrift at the bottom.

Club captain, Dave Merrington sent a letter to the *Burnley Express*. 'Points (have been) thrown away by individual mistakes,' it said; 'the players are 100% behind our manager, Mr Jimmy Adamson.' The chairman refused to contemplate any 'sudden dispensing of money we have carefully allocated for specific projects that have been planned for years'. Improvements to the Bee Hole End in the close season had cost £88,000 and Adamson had to rely on the players he had. The only moves were outward. Len Kinsella went to Carlisle United for £10,000 in September, and in the same month Wilf Wrigley decided to give up football in favour of studying geology at Aberystwyth University.

The reintroduction of Alan West and the debut of full back Eddie Cliff made little difference. Cliff was the ninth and final member of the 1968 Youth Cup side to make his debut. A side containing six of them went down 2–0 at Southampton, where Brian O'Neil had settled down well after his transfer in the summer.

The first win came in the 15th game, against Crystal Palace. Two goals by Eric Probert prompted Adamson to claim 'we will not go down'. But the following week Burnley crashed 4–0 at Tottenham. In the last five games at White Hart Lane, the Clarets had conceded a total of 22 goals without reply.

The return of Peter Mellor and Martin Dobson against Nottingham Forest at Turf Moor in November was overshadowed by the wonderful debut of Welsh winger Leighton James. Goals by Nulty and Probert gave Burnley a 2–1 victory, but any optimism was diffused when Ralph Coates damaged an ankle in training and was out for 4 weeks. His return was inauspicious as Burnley went down 4–0 at home to Manchester City.

After a 3–1 defeat at Newcastle, Dave Merrington, who was unable to secure a regular place in the side, resigned the captaincy and was succeeded by Martin Dobson who was an ever-present for the rest of the season.

The FA Cup offered no compensation. For the first time since 1958 Burnley went out to a lower division club – a 3–0 defeat at Second Division, Oxford United. Ronnie Welch came into the team for the 1–1 draw with Newcastle United which earned Burnley's sixth point in seven league games and put them only a point from safety. One point from the next three games raised them above Blackpool, but left them five points behind West Ham in 20th place (only two clubs were to be relegated).

For the away match at Crystal Palace in late February, Geoff Nulty partnered Waldron in the centre of defence allowing Dobson to get forward. Goals by Dobson and Coates gave Burnley their second win of the season over Palace and the first away win. The second came at Huddersfield a fortnight later thanks to a Colin Waldron goal.

The previous week, Paul Fletcher, a 20-year-old centre forward, had been signed from Bolton Wanderers for a club record fee of £60,000. It was the end of a long search for a forward – Adamson claimed that the club had looked at 34 others, but were either unable or unwilling to purchase them. Fletcher was not an immediate success, and Burnley dropped two more points in home draws with

Spurs and Ipswich. Waldron's penalty miss against Ipswich was the team's seventh failure in ten attempts. Burnley were further demoralised by a 4–0 thrashing at Leeds (Alan Clarke getting all four).

However, two wins over fellow-strugglers at Easter offered a last chance. Fletcher's first goal for the club earned a victory over Blackpool and a Geoff Nulty effort against West Ham put Burnley four points behind the London club with a game in hand. There were only five games to go and a win at Coventry was vital. Adamson opted for experience, fielding a team with Waiters, Angus, Latcham, Bellamy, Coates and Casper. The first half was goalless, but 8 minutes into the second half, a speculative 40-yard lob by Ernie Hunt deceived Waiters, and two late goals by City ensured that defeat at Championship-chasing Arsenal would send Burnley into the Second Division.

Mellor was recalled to the side, which was without Coates on international duty. A 25th minute penalty by Charlie George was enough to seal Burnley's fate. Jimmy Adamson blamed 'too much tension and anxiety after a bad start', and he cited Dobson's broken leg as the most significant factor in a very disappointing season. Bob Lord was quick to issue a vote of confidence in the manager, and he called relegation a 'temporary setback rather than a permanent disaster'.

The youth policy was obviously still functioning well. The Burnley team reached the semi-finals of the FA Youth Cup, and as many of this side would reach the first team as that of 1968. The line-up that lost to Cardiff City after a replay (1–3) was:

Parton

Welch   Wilson

Ingham   McMahon   Rodaway

Bradshaw   Falconer   Brennan   James   Morris

Full back Harry Wilson made his senior debut in the penultimate game at Chelsea, which was won with a Steve Kindon goal. Three days later at Wolves, Burnley suffered their 22nd defeat of the season and only Coates looked like a First Division player. He was the only one to remain so, as the following week, he was transferred to

Tottenham Hotspur for £190,000. Relegation had made his transfer inevitable. 'We did not want to sell him,' said Adamson; 'we had to sell him.'

His was not the only departure from Burnley during the close season. Ray Ternent was sold to Southend United and Rod Jones to Rochdale. Free transfers were given to Dave Merrington (he went to Bristol City), Les Latcham (to Plymouth Argylle), Peter Jones (to Swansea City) and Dave Wilson (to Chesterfield).

The plans for the £400,000 entertainments complex were 'temporarily shelved'. Bob Lord announced the board's view that 'if our priorities are put in the correct order, then emphasis should be placed on regaining our rightful place in the First Division. This may take money – therefore, further developments requiring capital may have to be postponed'.

There were no new players for the opening game at Cardiff, Burnley's first match in Division Two for 25 seasons. Alan West took over Coates' midfield role in a team of:

Waiters

Angus   Waldron   Dobson   Wilson

Bellamy   West   Thomas

Casper   Fletcher   Kindon

Dave Thomas starred and inspired a second-half fightback when switched to outside left. Goals by Casper and Dobson earned the draw.

John Angus played his 438th and last league game for Burnley in the win over Luton Town, and another playing career ended when Tony Waiters was rested after defeat at Oxford. Waiters resumed his coaching career, going to Coventry City in December and he was replaced by Peter Mellor.

League form was encouraging. Two goals by James at Fulham and a home win over Queens Park Rangers in mid-September put Burnley into third place. Arthur Bellamy's first hat-trick since 1963 helped the side to a 6–1 victory over Orient, and maintained the push for promotion.

In the League Cup, Burnley dismissed First Division Coventry City, and in the next round were drawn against Manchester United.

Leighton James gave the Clarets the lead at Old Trafford, but a Bobby Charlton goal forced a replay at Turf Moor, where another Charlton effort eventually put United through. Such was James' form that he became the youngest ever Burnley international, at 18, when selected for Wales against Czechoslovakia. Two 3–0 wins over Carlisle and. Cardiff respectively kept Burnley in fourth position, but they were on the wrong end of a similar scoreline at leaders, Norwich City.

Peter Mellor never regained the form that had brought him representative honours before his shoulder injury, and his place was taken for two games by Jeff Parton, at 18 Burnley's youngest post-war goalkeeper. He was unable to stop the slide and three defeats in four games left Burnley in eighth place in the middle of December. Jim Thomson returned to the side after an absence of 14 months in the troublesome left back position. One letter to the local press suggested 'a replacement in the Keith Newton mould'. The writer would only have to wait a further 5 months.

In the new year (1972), Burnley were ten points off the lead and an FA Cup run was hoped for to keep up interest in a flagging season. Mellor had another poor game, and Burnley went down 1–0 to First Division strugglers, Huddersfield Town. This was Mellor's last game for the Clarets, as the following week Adamson spent £50,000 on 21-year-old Chesterfield keeper, Alan Stevenson. Mellor went on loan to Chesterfield before being sold to Fulham for £25,000.

Alan West was called up to the England under–23 squad in January, but the general decline continued. Cries of 'Adamson Out' greeted the home defeat by Hull City in February and two Easter setbacks (4–2 at Blackpool and 4–3 at Sunderland) increased the pressure on the manager.

Eric Probert had been out of favour following a club suspension in December, but his return to the team sparked off a revival. A midfield of Probert, Dobson and new boy, Billy Ingham inspired victory in all of the last seven matches of the season. Burnley finished in a respectable seventh position and had scored enough goals to qualify for the following season's Watney Cup. In the penultimate game at home to Preston North End, 18-year-old central defender Billy Rodaway made his debut in a team which had seven members under 21. Once again the young players were a great cause for optimism as a team led by Harry Wilson won a five nation international youth tournament (James scored five of Burnley's seven goals).

The dwindling crowds in the second half of the season (only 8,663 to watch the game with Watford in mid-April) increased speculation as to the future of Dave Thomas, especially when he was not selected for the last seven games of the season. Despite being out of favour at Turf Moor, he was selected by Sir Alf Ramsey for the England under–23 squad. Thomas was unhappy about his position at Burnley and was placed on the transfer list.

Another player who did not now fit into future plans was Steve Kindon, who had had a very disappointing season. He had never quite lived up to his great early potential, and in June was sold to Wolverhampton Wanderers for £100,000. Arthur Bellamy went to Chesterfield for £10,000 and John Angus finally announced his retirement. Harry Potts, too, parted company with the club on the 'amicable terms' of £28,125 compensation.

The only new arrival was, as previously hoped for, Keith Newton. He was picked up on a free transfer from Everton. Holder of eighteen England caps, he had cost £90,000 from Blackburn Rovers two and a half years previously, but had been unable to regain his first team place after injury. His signing provided much-needed experience, and prompted Jimmy Adamson to claim 'I think we'll be among the promotion contenders', but in the pre-season Watney Cup there was little to support this view. A late James goal brought victory at Lincoln, but Burnley flopped at home, losing 2–0 to Third Division Bristol City.

Adamson's optimism was not widely shared and a crowd of only 9,804 turned up for the opening game at Turf Moor against Carlisle United. Eric Probert injured his right leg in a pre-season game and his midfield role was given to the transfer-listed Dave Thomas, who scored the second Burnley equaliser. After another draw, at Fulham, the first victory came with a 4–1 thrashing of Aston Villa at Turf Moor with the team:

Stevenson

Docherty   Waldron   Thomson   Newton

Thomas   Dobson   Collins

Casper   Fletcher   James

Further wins over Preston and Portsmouth took Burnley to the top of the table and earned Adamson a gallon of scotch as Bell's Whisky Second Division Manager of the Month. A four-goal lead was almost squandered in the home game with Blackpool, but the Clarets managed to hang on 4–3. A superb equalising goal at Luton by Leighton James kept Burnley as the only unbeaten team in the league.

In the same game, Thomas was substituted after only 31 minutes. It was to be his last appearance as the following week he was sold to promotion rivals, Queens Park Rangers for £165,000. Almost immediately, the chairman announced that work was to start on the new £200,000 stand. He had claimed in August that the board had 'cold feet about the money to be spent on the stand' but the sale of Thomas 2 months later gave them the confidence to proceed.

Adamson could not just go out and buy a successor to Thomas. 'The difficulty is,' he complained, 'the players worth £100,000 won't come to Burnley.' Thomas' place was therefore taken by Geoff Nulty and there was no change in form. James' goal at Sheffield Wednesday in October completed a fine team effort and a Paul Fletcher hat-trick clinched a victory over Cardiff. In November, the unbeaten run was extended to 22 games with a 3–3 draw at Middlesbrough, where two goals in the last 10 minutes by Fletcher and Dobson salvaged a point.

The following week the run came to an end with a 2–1 home defeat by third-from-bottom Orient. Dobson gave Burnley a first half lead, but was injured and failed to appear for the second period. He returned in the next game, at Brighton and his near post header prompted a run of four successive 1–0 victories which put Burnley four points clear at the top.

For the first game of 1973, Billy Ingham came in for the suspended Collins. It was the first change since the sale of Thomas, but the fine form continued with a memorable 3–0 victory at Aston Villa (goals by Newton, Nulty and Ingham). Ingham retained his place for the FA Cup tie with Liverpool. Burnley achieved a 0–0 draw but were powerless to prevent the First Division leaders winning the replay 3–0 at Anfield. It was Burnley's second cup defeat by a major team – having lost 4–0 at Leeds in the League Cup in early September.

For the top-of-the-table clash with QPR the Burnley supporters were the first to use the 'League Liner', a special football train with thirteen coaches, including a discotheque and a four-screen cinema, which was an attempt to curb hooliganism on long train journeys. The travelling fans saw their team lose their unbeaten away record and QPR close the gap at the top to just one point.

Defeat at home by Sheffield Wednesday in March knocked the Clarets off the top of the table, but a Frank Casper goal at Cardiff City restored Burnley's lead and a 4–0 victory over Portsmouth opened up a three-point gap.

There was a setback at Nottingham Forest, where Burnley were outplayed and lost for only the fourth time in the whole season, but a win at Huddersfield was the first of five consecutive April victories. Mick Docherty was injured in this game and declared himself 'sick as a parrot at missing out on all the glory at the end of the season'. His replacement, Ingham, had already deputised for Collins and Fletcher, and now played at right back against Sunderland, where two goals by Fletcher ensured promotion in front of a crowd of 22,896.

The series of wins left the side needing only a draw from the final match to clinch the title. The game was at Preston, who needed a point to be sure of avoiding relegation. Preston went ahead just before half time, but a 35-yard drive from Colin Waldron in the 53rd minute ensured that both sides got the point they required. Preston were safe and Burnley were the Champions of Division Two.

The season was closed with a testimonial game for John Angus. Many of his old colleagues returned to pay tribute to him. These included Jimmy Robson, who was subsequently signed on a free transfer from Bury as a 'youth development player', to play alongside the young reserves. (The appointment was not a success and Robson was released a year later.)

In July, Eddie Cliff and Eric Probert were sold to Notts County for a combined sum of £35,000. At the end of the previous season, Probert had appeared to be an integral part of Burnley's future, but he never regained his place after his pre-season injury. It was indicative of the solidity of the first team that he had made only one appearance (and that as substitute) all season. The only signing to strengthen the squad for the forthcoming season was that of Peter Noble, signed from Swindon Town for £35,000. He was regarded primarily as a striker, but was to prove himself just as important in various other positions.

For the 1973 Charity Shield versus Manchester City at Maine Road in August, Adamson kept faith with his Second Division Championship winning team and another Waldron effort clinched the trophy. Although favourites for relegation, Burnley began well with a 2–0 win at Sheffield United. Goals from Collins and Dobson gave the

Clarets victory and an injury to Mick Docherty meant that Noble's first appearance was at right back and he retained this position for most of the season. This made the line-up for the 1–0 win over Chelsea at Turf Moor:

Stevenson

Noble   Waldron   Thomson   Newton

Nulty   Dobson   Collins

Casper   Fletcher   James

Despite Burnley's reputation, only one of this side (James) had come through the youth policy. The other ten had been bought for the bargain sum of £269,000. This shows Adamson's new reliance on experience and shrewd purchasing. Of the 1968 Youth Cup team, only Docherty and West remained on the playing staff. Adamson's 'Team of the Seventies' had failed to materialise, but in its absence, he had built a very competent substitute.

James was joined by another youth product, Ray Hankin, when Fletcher was injured. Hankin had made one appearance as substitute the previous season, but made his full debut in the 3–2 victory at Spurs that put Burnley into second place in Division One. After Casper was carried off with a leg injury in the home draw with Spurs in September, Hankin and Fletcher formed a new 'Double Spearhead'. It was immediately effective. In the match against East Fife in the Texaco Cup, a Fletcher hat-trick helped Burnley to a 7–0 victory. The first league defeat came in the eighth game, at Ipswich, but the Clarets recovered well to beat Manchester City 3–0 and a Colin Waldron goal gave Burnley their first win at West Ham since 1961.

Alan West, who hadn't started a league game since the 1971–72 season, was transferred to Luton Town in October for £100,000. A move to Sunderland earlier in the season had fallen through on medical grounds. Another £60,000 was obtained by the sale of Ronnie Welch and Harry Wilson to Brighton in December. None of these players featured in the first team plans and the cash was vital in a winter of power shortages.

The semi-final of the Texaco Cup against Norwich City had to be played on a midweek afternoon and attracted only 4,915 spectators.

To counter this, the club bought its own generator for £30,000. This did not prove a great success. Bob Lord described a crowd of 18,815 at Turf Moor against Sheffield United in January as a 'kick in the teeth' for the club. He had expected 25,000, but many people were forced to work on Saturdays that winter and some thought the chairman's remarks insulting. Tact was not Lord's strong point. He had long been an opponent of too much TV soccer (the last game shown from Turf Moor was in August 1972). At a dinner in March he asserted that 'we have to stand up against a move to get soccer on the cheap by the Jews who run television'. He did apologise for his remarks, but it did lead to strained relations with other clubs (the Leeds United chairman Manny Cussins, a Jew himself, banned Lord from the directors' box at Elland Road).

Champions Liverpool came to Turf Moor on Boxing Day and an 85th minute goal by Hankin gave the Clarets a 2–1 victory. A draw against Wolves the following Saturday kept Burnley in third place and gave them a playing record in all matches for 1973 of:

P	W	D	L	F	A	P
52	31	12	9	92	46	74

Recognition of the team's achievements was increasing. James was a regular international, whilst Dobson had earned a call-up to the full England squad and both Stevenson and Fletcher had been selected at under–23 level.

In the third round of the FA Cup, goals by Newton and Hankin gave a 2–1 win at Grimsby and a superb performance by James inspired a 4–1 victory at Oldham in the next round. This was James' last game before suspension. His replacement was Brian Flynn, the diminutive Welsh midfielder, who made his debut at Arsenal in February in a 4–4–2 formation. Noble played as a striker partnering Fletcher with Billy Ingham at right back.

The new stand on Brunshaw Road was first used for the home defeat by Ipswich Town on 9 February. The following week was the fifth round of the FA Cup. A Paul Fletcher goal was enough to defeat Aston Villa. A similar scoreline was achieved in the sixth round against Third Division, Wrexham. In front of a crowd of 36,091 a Frank Casper goal ensured a semi-final place.

League form was suffering. There had not been a win in the league since Boxing Day. Micky Finn made his debut in the goals at Chelsea in March, but could not prevent a 3–0 defeat. Stevenson's return in the next match coincided with victory over Everton, where three goals in 4 minutes gave Burnley a 3–1 victory.

The week before the semi-final, Burnley inflicted the only home defeat of the season on Champions-elect, Leeds United (the banned Burnley chairman chose to watch a game at Blackpool). In a devastating performance Burnley ran out 4–1 winners. Paul Fletcher got two of the goals, including a stunning overhead effort. Casper received a knock from Norman Hunter, but was declared fit for the semi-final against Newcastle United.

55,000 packed into Hillsborough and saw Geoff Nulty head against the bar in the first half with Burnley on top. But in the second half, neither Waldron nor Thomson could contain Malcolm MacDonald. Twice he raced through the Burnley defence to beat Stevenson and put Newcastle into the final.

League form was still inconsistent. Debutant Ian Brennan conceded a penalty in a 4–0 defeat at Stoke. But five points from three games at Easter kept alive hopes of qualifying for Europe. Burnley's last two games of the season were against their semi-final opponents, Newcastle United. Two wins would secure both the Texaco Cup and a place in the UEFA Cup. Fletcher put Burnley into the lead in the one-legged Texaco Cup final at St James' Park. But Burnley's scourge, MacDonald equalised and captain, Bobby Moncur got the winner in extra time. Another MacDonald goal (equalised by Fletcher) deprived Burnley of a vital point in the league at Turf Moor. Stoke won their last match and thus got into the UEFA Cup, where they were drawn against Ajax of Amsterdam, one of the top teams in Europe. Burnley had just missed out on potential European glory which could have brought in much-needed revenue. Nonetheless, they had started the season as relegation favourites but finished it in sixth position, and a team including 18-year-old midfielder Bobby Flavell won the third place play-off in the FA Cup at Leicester thanks to a goal by Hankin.

After the last game with Newcastle, the Turf Moor pitch was dug up, and a new surface was laid at a cost of £60,000. It was also announced that new £30,000 floodlights were to be installed to bring them up to UEFA standard. For the new season (1974–75), family season tickets were introduced for the Cricket Field Stand. These tickets, which worked out cheaper than buying separate ones, proved popular, and by June ticket sales were 2,000 up on the previous season.

There was obviously widespread optimism about the near future, but much of this was dispelled by the publication of the previous year's accounts. The main expenditure of the financial year (up to 31 March 1974) had been the replacement of the stand at a cost of £209,365. Largely as a consequence of this, the club announced a loss of £224,376. There was only one way to make good this loss. After only three games of the new season Martin Dobson was sold to Everton for £300,000. Bob Lord saw the deal as 'the latest step in a policy which is keeping Burnley in the First Division'. But a disgruntled supporter asked poignantly in the local press: 'Do we want a successful side or *the best ground in the Fourth Division*?' The rest of the board had put forward plans to name the new stand after the chairman, but to many disillusioned fans it became known as 'The Martin Dobson Stand'. The new stand increased the overall capacity to 42,000, more than double the average gate, but Bob Lord insisted that 'stand members should be able to sit and watch the game from a side view'. For the sake of a better view, he was willing to sell the club captain and jeopardise the potential of a promising side.

The season had not begun well. The first win did not come until the last day of August (4 days after Dobson's departure) in the fifth game. A 3–0 win over Coventry was achieved under Waldron's captaincy with a team of:

Stevenson

Newton   Waldron   Rodaway   Brennan

Ingham   Noble   Collins

Hankin   Fletcher   James

This started a four-match winning run, which ruled out any immediate need to strengthen the squad. The run included a 2–1 home victory over Leeds United on 14 September, when ex-Prime Minister, Edward Heath officially opened 'The Bob Lord Stand'. He witnessed a fiery contest, in which Hankin and Gordon McQueen, the Leeds centre half, were dismissed for fighting. Underneath the stand a £60,000 social club was constructed. The 'Centre Spot', as it was called, was opened in November by Matt Busby and Tom Finney.

The sequence of wins came to an end at Derby, but Burnley came back well with a 1–0 victory at Liverpool. Flynn came in for Hankin with Noble moving into the attack, but it was a 35-yard effort from Ian Brennan that gave the first Burnley win at Anfield for 12 years. Brian Flynn earned a call-up into the full Welsh squad after only five senior games, and his compatriot, James was putting in world-class displays, most notably against Manchester United in the 3–2 League Cup defeat at Old Trafford. A Fletcher goal against Ipswich Town put Burnley sixth in the table in mid-October, but six games without a win saw them slipping down the table. The slide was halted by a Peter Noble hat-trick against one of his old clubs, Newcastle United. On their journey back bricks were thrown at the Newcastle team coach, one of which struck Newcastle striker John Tudor on the head. This was the worst example of the increasing amount of crowd disorder associated with the game. Outbreaks of fighting on the terraces had become almost commonplace.

In the absence of Dobson, Doug Collins was playing the key mid-field role and he inspired Burnley to a 3–0 win over QPR, which took them into seventh position only three points behind the leaders. The depth of midfield talent (Collins, Noble, Flynn, Ingham) persuaded the management to accept Newcastle United's offer of £120,000 for Geoff Nulty, who had not started a senior game since August. The transfer in December meant that the club had topped £2 million in post-war sales.

The 1975 FA Cup draw, at home to Southern League, Wimbledon, seemed to offer, according to Jimmy Adamson, 'a wonderful opportunity to make progress'. But Wimbledon's plan to shut out James and Collins worked well and a 49th minute goal by Mick Mahon gave them a deserved 1–0 victory. It was the first time for 55 years that a non-league team had won on a First Division team's ground in the FA Cup.

Although Adamson pronounced it a 'shattering blow to our pride', it seemed to have a favourable effect on league form. Colin Morris, a young winger who had come on as substitute in the Wimbledon game, made his full debut at QPR, where a Ray Hankin goal clinched victory. Billy Ingham's effort at home to Luton Town the following week was enough to put Burnley into third place just a point off the top.

Victory over Sheffield United put Burnley into second place and a 3–0 win at Coventry in March increased their hopes of the Championship. A home draw with Liverpool and defeat at West Ham deflated these hopes, but the main blow came when Paul Fletcher had to go into hospital for a cartilage operation after the West Ham game. With Casper still out (his injury had recently necessitated a third operation), the attack lacked bite. Billy Rodaway and Billy Ingham were tried up front, as was debutant, Derrick Parker but none made sufficient impact. The defence too was suffering towards the end of the season. Stevenson was dropped after a 5–2 defeat at Derby, but Finn could do little better letting in four at Carlisle. There were debuts for full back Derek Scott and central defender Richard Dixey, but Burnley faded badly and despite being leading scorers with 68 goals finished only in tenth place.

'Success did not come,' claimed Adamson, 'because we did not have the strength in depth in our squad.' He reiterated his aim to buy rather than sell and was supported in this by his chairman's new attitude.

'We do not need the money from big money transfers to enable us to run Burnley Football Club,' stated Bob Lord in May 1975. 'Of all the money we have received, seven-eighths of the total has been spent on improvements. Any suggestion that we have to sell to survive is sheer nonsense.'

Plans were put forward to get £250,000 a year from the development association (it currently provided under £60,000). The lottery was to be enlarged and sponsorship of matches was introduced. Pop concerts were also planned. Seating on the Longside and the covering of the Bee Hole End remained long-term objectives, but with the two new stands now complete, the emphasis was placed on the playing side.

The squad was indeed strengthened. Gerry Peyton, a young goalkeeper, came from Southern League, Atherstone, for £5,000, and two 30-year old ex-internationals, Mike Summerbee and Willie Morgan, were also signed. Summerbee was bought from Manchester City and on the same day (10 June) Morgan rejoined his old club for £32,000 (£5,000 more than Summerbee) from Manchester United. The double signing shows another stage (after Newton and Noble) in the plans to add experience to the squad. Both Morgan and Summerbee were best known as wingers and this inevitably increased speculation as to the future of Leighton James. But Adamson was only interested in enlarging his first team pool and he assured supporters that 'Leighton James is stopping at Burnley'. The club announced a profit of £194,000, which fostered the belief that the club could hang on to

James; the prospect of his linking up with the old Burnley favourite, Willie Morgan, caught the public imagination and for the first time ever season ticket sales brought in over £100,000.

Adamson's hyperbole of 5 years before remained unfulfilled, but there appeared to be a promising future. Burnley may not have been 'The Team of the Seventies', but Bob Lord summed up the general attitude, when he said, 'We feel we are now established as a top-class First Division club . . . this could be our year.'

1974–75 – Division One

Back: *Miller, Thomson, Newton, Hankin, Stevenson, Brennan, Fletcher, Rodaway, Brown*
Front: *Collins, Nulty, Docherty, Noble, Adamson, Waldron, Ingham, Casper, James*

(Photograph © The Burnley Express)

1978–79 – Division Two

Back: Robertson, Gardiner, McGregor, Kindon, Overson(R), McAdam, Arins, Pashley
2nd: Holland, Potts, Casper, Burke, Jakub, Brennan, O'Rourke, Reynolds, Stevenson, Norman, Robinson, Dixon, Higgins, Miller, Pointer
3rd: Hall, Ingham, Smith, Rodaway, Noble, Fletcher, Thomson, Morley, Scott, Cochrane
Front: Anderson, Wardrobe, Walker, Pickerill, Wharton, McBride, Young, Cavener, Laws, Tait, Gray, Overson(V)

(Photograph © The Burnley Express)

Chapter 5

Internal Decline

(16 August 1975–12 April 1980)

The 1975–76 season opened with an unimpressive goalless draw with Arsenal at Turf Moor. The Burnley team, in a new strip of claret shirts with a large blue 'V' was:

Stevenson

Docherty   Waldron   Thomson   Newton

Morgan   Noble   Collins

Summerbee   Hankin   James

Despite the talk of two wingers, Morgan was played in a midfield role. He suffered an arm injury, and his place was taken by Brian Flynn for another home draw, with Everton. Morgan was played on the right wing at home to Middlesbrough and proved a revelation. Peter Noble grabbed a hat-trick in a 4–1 victory which seemed to justify much of the pre-season optimism.

Hopes of further progress were dashed by some poor defensive displays. Eleven goals were conceded in three consecutive games: a 3–0 defeat at Champions, Derby County; a 4–4 home draw with Norwich City in which Noble scored all four; and a 4–0 loss at Birmingham City, where Doug Collins broke his leg. The injury situation worsened a few days later, when Ian Brennan, recently restored to the team, also suffered a broken leg – in a car accident. Further defeats by bottom of the table Sheffield United and by Leeds United put Burnley in 19th position at the end of September.

A defensive improvement led to a 2–1 win at Coventry and a 1–1 draw at Anfield in the third round of the League Cup. A Peter Noble penalty won the replay, and the general situation seemed to be improving. Frank Casper returned to the team after an absence of seven months on 18 October, and his late winner against QPR was his 100th goal in league football. Paul Fletcher made an encouraging comeback the following week in a 1–1 draw at Aston Villa, which was Burnley's sixth consecutive game unbeaten (all in October).

November proved a disastrous month. Despite a League Cup victory over Leicester City, Burnley lost five successive league games – including a humiliating 5–1 home defeat by Wolves. The club also lost its star player, Leighton James. After the game with Wolves he put in a transfer request and on 28 November he was sold to Derby County for £310,000. 'It's ambition . . . which makes me leave Burnley,' he told a local reporter. His desire to join a successful club shattered many of the illusions about Burnley's hopes and condemned the rest of the season to a fight against relegation. His initial replacement was Paul Bradshaw, who made his full debut in the 1–0 defeat at QPR. Another London defeat (at Spurs) kept Burnley in the relegation zone.

Burnley also went out of the League Cup – losing 2–0 at home to Middlesbrough. After this game, Stevenson was dropped in favour of Gerry Peyton, who made a remarkable debut in the goalless draw with Liverpool at Turf Moor. Also making his debut in midfield was Kevin Kennerley. He scored the following week to give victory over West Ham, but three more defeats kept Burnley in trouble.

The club's hopes switched to the FA Cup, but in a stormy third round tie, the Clarets went down 1–0 at Blackpool. The board decided action had to be taken, and the following Tuesday Jimmy Adamson was asked to resign. His assistant, Joe Brown, was appointed in a move that proved unpopular with some of the senior professionals – most notably Waldron and vice-captain Collins. In Brown's first game in charge, David Loggie was brought into the team to lead the attack against Norwich (1–3). Mick Docherty was dropped for the game with Derby and the job of marking Leighton James on his return to Turf Moor fell to Derek Scott. He could not prevent the Welsh winger scoring and defeat left Burnley in 21st place.

Colin Morris made his first appearance of the season at Everton and inspired a 3–2 victory. Despite his confident performance, another winger was purchased the following week. England under–23 international, Tony Morley was signed from Preston North End for £100,000. This was a record fee for Burnley, beating the £60,000 paid for Fletcher. The deals had certain similarities – an inexperienced striker bought to stave off relegation. Like Fletcher,

Morley made his Burnley debut at Turf Moor, against Ipswich Town – and, as six years previously, Burnley lost 1–0 and remained in 21st place.

Frank Casper's attempted return proved unsuccessful and he announced his retirement. He was appointed youth team trainer. Other experienced players were declared surplus to requirements. Collins, Morgan, Docherty and Stevenson were all placed on the transfer list. Only Morgan went before the transfer deadline – to Bolton Wanderers on a free transfer. The expectation of a James-Morgan wing partnership had only been fulfilled on one occasion (at home to Middlesbrough) and both players had departed before the end of the season which had promised so much.

Doug Collins was recalled for the goalless draw with Manchester City, where Peyton saved a Dennis Tueart penalty, which kept Burnley only a point from safety. Collins was suspended the following week after publishing an article in *Weekly News* where he claimed he was playing for himself, and not the club, making it clear that he wanted to leave. Defeats by Spurs, Liverpool and Leeds left Burnley with little chance of survival, but Ray Hankin's goal against fellow-strugglers, Birmingham City kept the slim hopes alive. Another 1–0 victory, at Newcastle, was achieved with a goal from Noble, but defeat by the same scoreline at Turf Moor by Manchester United on 19 April sent Burnley into the Second Division.

The board was quick to give the manager a vote of confidence, and he soon completed his clear-out. Despite a financial loss for that year of £146,871, no money was collected for the transfers of Collins to Plymouth Argylle, Waldron to Manchester United, Docherty to Manchester City and Kennerley to Port Vale. The scouting system, for so long a lifeline for the club was also cut – nine of the part-time scouts were dismissed. Chief Scout, Dave Blakey was most unhappy about the situation and resigned to take up a similar position at Sheffield Wednesday.

New club captain, Keith Newton picked up a heel injury in pre-season training and in the opening game on 21 August 1976, Terry Pashley took his place. Pashley had made his debut against Birmingham City the previous season and now formed a teenage full-back partnership with Derek Scott. Tony Morley, who in the close season had had his head shaved, also missed the start of the season, with an eye injury. This meant the reintroduction of Paul Bradshaw, who played in the opening goalless draw at Wolverhampton. Bradshaw scored at Turf Moor against Fulham in the 3–1 win and again 4 days later against Luton Town, but Burnley still went down 2–1.

Another defeat was suffered in the League Cup at the hands of Fourth Division Torquay United, where ex-Claret Willie Brown scored the only goal. A Dixie MacNeil hat-trick at Hereford put Burnley into 15th position. Bob Lord had said that 'the management know that the team needs strengthening', but now announced that he was prepared to let two players go. Ray Hankin, still only 20, was sold to Leeds United for £180,000 and Paul Bradshaw went to Sheffield Wednesday for £20,000. Two players were signed – Malcolm Smith (on loan from Middlesbrough) and Terry Cochrane from Coleraine. Cochrane, who had previously been on loan, was signed for £28,000 and he scored on his debut at home to Orient. The team, which obtained the 3–3 draw in this game, was:

Stevenson

Scott   Thomson   Rodaway   Pashley

Noble   Flynn

Cochrane   Smith   Fletcher   Morley

The defence continued badly – in the next two games, the recalled Peyton let in nine goals: 4–1 down to Charlton Athletic, Burnley fought back to draw; and a 5–2 defeat at Notts Forest put Burnley into the relegation zone. For the next game, Stevenson, Brennan, Newton, Ingham and Summerbee were restored to the side and the new 4–4–2 system achieved two 1–0 victories against Plymouth Argylle and Oldham Athletic respectively.

The rapid decline in the club's fortunes and the failure to spend more of the £200,000 acquired from transfers led to increasing opposition to the board's policies. The first cries of 'Bob Lord Out' were greeted by a firm refusal from the chairman – 'The only thing that could make me resign is my death.' A protest march and 5,000-signature petition calling for his resignation caused Lord to announce the dire financial position – the club was £400,000 in debt and making a weekly loss of over £4,000. He claimed the club was on the verge of bankruptcy and that he was prepared to sell Brian Flynn.

Nevertheless, the club refused an offer of £25,000 from a local pools winner, Danny Carr, in order to purchase Malcolm Smith, who had scored six goals during his 2 months' loan. The slight improvement in form with the introduction of the 4–4–2 system quietened both the criticism of the chairman and Lord's scare stories over club finances. Some money was obtained in December from the sale of Gerry Peyton to Fulham for £40,000 and the Turf Moor gym was put up for sale for £50,000. (Other departures later in the season included Colin Morris and Derrick Parker to Southend United for a combined sum of £13,000 and Mike Summerbee to Blackpool on a free transfer). Jack Butterfield, the Commercial Director, declared himself dissatisfied with the running of the club – he saw the give-away of experienced players in the close season and the refusal of the £25,000 offered for Smith as lost financial opportunities and he resigned from his post in December.

Doug Collins returned to Turf Moor on 3 January (1977) and his Plymouth side won 2–0, sending Burnley into the relegation zone. Two games were needed to dismiss Lincoln City in the third round of the FA Cup, but a dreadful display at Third Division, Port Vale, in the next round resulted in a 2–1 defeat. The anti-Bob Lord 'Supporters' Association' attempted to organise a boycott of the home game with Hereford on 12 February, but 8,748 still turned up to witness the 1–1 draw. Two away defeats – at Oldham and Southampton – took Burnley to 21st position; increased the run without a league win to 14 matches; and earned Joe Brown the sack. In his 13 months in charge, the club had dropped an entire division and had won only nine of 45 matches.

Brown was succeeded by Harry Potts, who had been chief scout since the resignation of Dave Blakey in July. A 4–2–4 formation was restored and it worked immediately. Goals by Cochrane and Noble against Carlisle United ensured Burnley's first league win for 4 months. However, defensive frailties were exposed in two more away defeats – 1–5 at Notts County and 1–4 at Hull City. Jim Thomson was dropped in favour of Peter Robinson, who had made his debut the previous November. A 1–0 victory was achieved over Sheffield United at Turf Moor. Billy Ingham came into the team for Cochrane at Orient, which meant a 4–3–3 formation which gained Burnley's second away win of the season. At Turf Moor, however, Notts Forest gained a 1–0 victory through a goal by Tony Woodcock (Burnley had tried to sign Woodcock the previous year, but had been unable to raise the £15,000 fee). Four points in three games at Easter put Burnley into 18th position and the improvement was confirmed when a Billy Ingham goal beat leaders Chelsea. The danger of relegation was not finally removed until the final home game of the season: Tony Morley scored his first two goals for the club in the 3–1 victory over Notts County. A 2–0 defeat at Millwall meant that Burnley finished in 16th position – better than had seemed likely at the turn of the year, but still rather disappointing.

Despite the disappointing form, there were no changes in the squad for the new season (1977–78), although the club revealed it was prepared to give Jim Thomson a free transfer. Peter Noble had replaced Keith Newton as club captain, and Newton later announced that he was to retire at the end of the season. Noble was injured in the League Cup victory at Chester and his place was taken by Scottish midfielder, Marshall Burke for the opening league game at home to Bolton Wanderers, in a team of:

Stevenson

Newton   Robinson   Rodaway   Brennan

Burke   Ingham   Flynn

Cochrane   Loggie   Morley

A 1–0 defeat was followed by a 3–0 reverse at Sunderland. Jimmy Adamson was in charge at Sunderland, and his team included Docherty and Waldron with Doug Collins as substitute. Another loss, at Stoke put Burnley at the bottom of the division.

Noble returned to lead the attack in the 3–1 League Cup victory over First Division, Norwich City, but in the league Crystal Palace subdued Cochrane and Morley and gained a draw at Turf Moor. England youth international, Rob Higgins, made his debut at centre half against Brighton, whilst Robinson was switched to centre forward without success in a goalless draw. Paul Fletcher returned after injury, but was sent off in the 4–1 defeat at Mansfield. Millwall won 2–0 in front of the lowest post-war Turf Moor crowd of 7,223 and Burnley were on the wrong end of another 4–1 scoreline at Fulham.

The recall of Jim Thomson against Bristol Rovers on 8 October coincided with the first league win of the season (3–1), but this did not prove a turning point. Only one point was gained from the next four league matches and Burnley were knocked out of the League Cup by Ipswich Town. After the cup tie, Brian Flynn was sold to

Leeds United for £170,000. Some of the money was spent immediately: Brian Hall, the ex-Liverpool midfielder was signed from
Plymouth Argylle for £25,000 and Steve Kindon returned to the
club from Wolves for £80,000. They made their debuts against Notts
County on 12 November, in the team:

Stevenson

Newton   Thomson   Rodaway   Brennan

Hall   Noble

Cochrane   Fletcher   Kindon   Morley

A goal by Kindon and two by Fletcher produced a morale-boosting
3–1 victory. The first away win was achieved 3 weeks later at Luton.
Cochrane was replaced by Ingham, and a more solid 4–3–3 formation
gave Burnley a 2–1 victory with the two new purchases as scorers.
The following week, the Clarets beat Charlton Athletic 1–0 and thus
caught the pack at the bottom of Division Two, having been five
points adrift 4 weeks previously. However, three successive defeats
ensured that they remained in 22nd place going into 1978.

The new year began well with a 2–1 win at Burnden Park, where
Bolton Wanderers had dropped only a point all season. Ian Brennan,
in a midfield role, got both the goals. In the FA Cup Fletcher scored
a late winner against Fulham at Turf Moor, and a further 1–0 win
over Stoke City the following week took Burnley off the bottom.
They remained in the relegation zone, however, as they did not win
another game for almost 2 months (including a 6–2 FA Cup defeat
at Chelsea).

Five wins in 16 days, starting with a 4–1 defeat of Sheffield United
at Turf Moor on 11 March, lifted Burnley into 15th position and
earned Harry Potts the Bell's Whisky Second Division Manager of
the Month award for March.

On the first day of April, Burnley ended Tottenham Hotspur's 19
game unbeaten sequence and a 4–2 win over Cardiff City extended
Burnley's own run to ten games. Two defeats in London (at Orient
and Charlton Athletic) ensured that relegation was still a possibility,
but the season ended with two home wins (over Fulham and Luton)
which secured for Burnley a place in the top half of the table.

Ten years after winning the FA Youth Cup, the club had another good run in the competition. The Burnley side reached the semi-finals against Aston Villa, but an ankle injury to England youth goalkeeper, Billy O'Rourke damaged their chances. His place was taken by a 16-year-old local schoolboy, Craig Carter, which left a team of:

Carter

D Tait   Dixon   J Tate   Young

Laws   Wharton   Robertson

Cavener   McGregor   Whittaker

In front of a crowd of 3,363 at Turf Moor, the side went down 3–1 in the first leg, and despite O'Rourke's return, they lost the second 1–0.

The 1978–79 season started promisingly with victories in the Anglo-Scottish Cup over Preston North End and Blackpool and a draw at Blackburn, which secured Burnley a two-legged tie with Glasgow Celtic in September. The season proper began with a 2–2 home draw with Leicester City, with the team:

Stevenson

Scott   Thomson   Rodaway   Brennan

Smith   Noble   Ingham

Cochrane   Fletcher   Kindon

This was the first of four consecutive draws, including a League Cup tie with Bradford City. In the replay Burnley fought back from 2–0 down to win 3–2. A similar result was achieved against West Ham the following Saturday, when Jim Thomson's first goal since 1973 put Burnley into fourth place in the league.

On the morning of the West Ham game, Burnley re-signed Leighton James from QPR for £165,000, and he played on the left side of midfield in the first leg of the Anglo-Scottish Cup quarter final against Premier League leaders, Celtic at Turf Moor. Steve Kindon's goal gave Burnley a 1–0 victory, but the result was overshadowed by crowd violence. The game had to be stopped in the 80th minute because of a pitch invasion caused largely by people getting out of the way of a bombardment of bottles, bricks and iron bars from rioting Celtic supporters. The fence segregating the two sets of fans, which had been erected in 1975, was ripped up and the fence posts used as weapons. The ensuing violence resulted in over 60 injuries. It was possible to restart the game, but much of the pleasure of victory was tarnished by the disturbance.

Burnley's 13-match unbeaten run was finally ended in a decisive 4–0 defeat at Sheffield United. The following week, Burnley lost again – to a nine-man Sunderland. The Wearsiders had Henderson and Bolton sent off in the 40th minute, but two second-half goals by Gary Rowell were enough to give them victory – a spectacular effort from Morley proved to be only a consolation.

For the second leg against Celtic at Parkhead, Potts adopted a 4–4–2 system and this counter-attacking style worked well as goals by Kindon and Brennan gave Burnley another win. The formation was successful again at Millwall 4 days later (2–0) and when a winger returned to the team, in the form of Cochrane, Burnley suffered a 3–1 reverse in the League Cup against Brighton. Cochrane was dropped to substitute for the home game with Oldham Athletic, and refused to go on when asked. He had recently won back his place in the Northern Ireland squad and was therefore unhappy at not securing a permanent place in the Burnley line-up. In October, he was transferred to Middlesbrough for £210,000. £50,000 of this went to Coleraine, which left Burnley with almost exactly what they had paid for Leighton James. A profit had been made on the sale of Terry Pashley to Blackpool (£30,000) and David Loggie to York City (£20,000).

Brian Hall was restored to the team for the league game with Brighton. James was played as a spare forward and he inspired a 3–0 victory. In the next league game an attempt to mark James out of the game by Crystal Palace's Kenny Sansom failed and Burnley were not flattered by a 2–1 scoreline. The Anglo-Scottish Cup semi-final against Mansfield Town had to be settled by a penalty shoot-out – the first at Turf Moor. With the penalty score at 7–6 to Mansfield, Derek Scott's kick hit the post, but the referee adjudged the goalkeeper was not on his line. Scott scored at the second attempt; Stevenson saved the next Mansfield effort; and Billy Rodaway put Burnley into the final against Oldham Athletic. In the first leg at Boundary Park, two goals (from Noble and Kindon) in the first 3 minutes effectively sealed the tie. Burnley ran out 4–1 winners and despite going down 1–0 at Turf Moor, won the 1978 Anglo-Scottish Cup.

Full back Tony Arins made his debut in a memorable 5–3 win over Fulham in November whilst Derek Scott was in hospital for an appendix operation (Scott had done his own selection chances no harm by marrying Brian Miller's daughter the month before). A hat-trick by Noble helped Burnley to within two points of the top of the table. Away form was slightly disappointing and despite further home victories over Bristol Rovers (two goals for Billy Ingham) and Blackburn, Burnley entered 1979 only in seventh position.

Tony Morley was recalled for the FA Cup third round tie at First Division Birmingham City and scored within a minute. A further goal for James in the closing stages gave Burnley a very creditable win and a home tie with Sunderland. It was a hard winter and the game was postponed on eight occasions. Originally scheduled for 27 January it was played on 21 February and a Jim Thomson goal earned a 1–1 draw. Such was the fixture congestion that Burnley featured in the sixth round draw – Ipswich Town or Bristol Rovers versus Liverpool or Burnley or Sunderland. They overcame Sunderland 3–0 in a great display at Roker Park, but the scoreline was reversed only 2 days later against the European Champions at Anfield. The following Saturday in their fifth game in 11 days, at Brighton, the Clarets went down again and had dropped to 15th position. The first league win of the year was achieved on 13 March against Luton Town, through two goals by Peter Noble. Morley's goal at Blackburn on Easter Saturday helped Burnley to seventh place, but they had lost too much ground on the leaders to challenge for promotion. Morley had come on as substitute at Ewood Park for Kindon, and was given an extended run in the team, showing at last much of his potential. Joe Jakub returned to the team after breaking his leg and there were debuts for midfield players, Kevin Young and Stuart Robertson. However, despite some fine individual performances, the side failed to win any of its last eight games and finished in 13th position. Only two goals were scored in this period and the last home game was watched by just 5,737 spectators. The management once again ignored the danger signs and in June, Morley was sold to Aston Villa for £220,000. His subsequent success at Villa (helping them to the European Cup in 1982) further illustrates the wasting of his talents at Turf Moor.

The trend of returns continued when the club re-signed Martin

Dobson, now 31, from Everton for £100,000 (Also, Arthur Bellamy was appointed the 'B' team coach). The strip was changed back to the claret shirts with blue sleeves of the 1960s (although with blue shorts and socks) and the team for the opening draw at Orient on 18 August 1979 was:

Stevenson

Scott   Thomson   Rodaway   Brennan

Ingham   Noble   Dobson

Kindon   Fletcher   James

Stevenson had made his debut for Burnley in 1972; this defence had played in the opening game of 1977; the midfield trio dated back to 1973; and the attack had played together as far back as October 1971. The 'Team of the Seventies' had been resurrected for one final attempt at immortality.

The Burnley public was sceptical of the prospects for a side which had had to fight against relegation in three of the previous four seasons and the opening Turf Moor attendance of 6,807 against Charlton Athletic reflected this. The low figure was also caused by the increase in ground admission to £1.50 (it was cheaper to watch Liverpool or Manchester United) and the abolition of concessionary rates for juveniles and pensioners. Owing to abuse of this system, the club offered reduced prices on season tickets only and apparently lost much support because of this.

The season started disastrously – in the first 11 games, the team failed to win and scored only nine goals. Kevin Young was reintroduced to the midfield in September, and Jeff Tate was brought in to lead the attack at Charlton Athletic, where a 3–3 draw was achieved. A 2–0 home defeat by Cardiff City on 13 October was the 24th competitive game without a win (dating back to Easter Saturday) and Harry Potts's last game in charge. As in 1970, he was persuaded by the board to stand down in favour of his chief coach. Brian Miller did not have the easiest start to his managerial career. His first game resulted in a 3–2 defeat at Preston North End, and the situation worsened when Stevenson suffered a strained knee. This necessitated a debut for Billy O'Rourke who had the misfortune to make his debut in front of the television cameras, but behind a dreadful defensive performance at QPR. A 7–0 defeat was no reflection on O'Rourke's form, as he made a number of good saves.

Paul Dixon and Vince Overson were brought in to shore up the defence (Vince's brother, Richard, was also briefly included in the first team). Two good draws were earned – 1–1 at Leicester and 0–0 at home to leaders, Luton Town. The first win of the season came on 24 November over a nine-man Cambridge United side. Cambridge had two men sent off in the 43rd minute, but still managed to stay level (at 3–3) until the 86th minute, when goals by James and Tate gave Burnley their first win in 7 months and 27 matches. Paul Fletcher, who had lost his confidence and had not scored all season, was substituted in the 82nd minute and did not play for Burnley again. The following week the club paid QPR £55,000 for the services of Northern Ireland centre forward, Billy Hamilton, whose debut was at Bristol Rovers, in a team of:

Stevenson

Arins   Overson (V)   Dixon   Brennan

Smith   Dobson   Burke   Young

James   Hamilton

Hamilton had the ball in the net after only 4 minutes – only to see it disallowed for a foul on the goalkeeper, but Burnley held on for a good point. The money spent on the striker was soon recouped as Steve Kindon was sold to Huddersfield Town for £50,000.

A Marshall Burke goal against Watford in early December took Burnley to within a point of the pack at the bottom of the table, and two 3–2 victories (over Newcastle United and Notts County, respectively) lifted them out of the relegation positions. The game at Notts County was notable for the emergence of the young winger Phil Cavener. He was thought to be as good a prospect as James had been, back in 1971. Brian Miller was chosen as Second Division Manager of the Month, and the club entered the new decade with a measure of optimism.

The changes that Miller had had to implement in order to improve the team's fortunes did not produce a sustained revival. He later acknowledged that the gruelling Christmas period had taken a lot out of some of the younger players, which makes the mid-January decision to sell Peter Noble more mysterious. Noble professed himself 'shocked and surprised' at Burnley's willingness to let him go, but he was transferred to Blackpool for £5,000 (he was joined there the following month by Paul Fletcher – sold for £30,000). Dobson took over the captaincy and scored the penalty which dismissed First Division Stoke City in the FA Cup third round. In the next round, the lower division side once again triumphed as Burnley went down 1–0 at Bury. Bottom of the table Fulham came to Turf Moor on 2 February and were beaten 2–1 – it was to prove Burnley's last win of the season.

Four goals by Stan Cummins produced a heavy defeat at Sunderland, and Miller began to see the inadequacies of his squad. Leighton James was put on the transfer list to help finance the purchase of Bobby Shinton, the Manchester City winger, for £200,000. Shinton, however, turned down the move and the only newcomer was Martyn Busby on a month's loan from QPR. He was signed, according to the manager, 'to give the young lads in midfield a rest' (a role for which Peter Noble would have been suited).

Busby's arrival coincided with a recurrence of Martin Dobson's achilles tendon injury, which kept him out for the rest of the season. Busby himself was stretchered off in only his second game, but returned on 15 March at Chelsea. He scored, but could not prevent a 2–1 defeat which left the Clarets 4 points behind Watford and the safety of 19th position, with only nine games to go. Busby was keen for a permanent move at the end of his loan period, but Burnley would only offer another month and he returned to QPR.

Thomson and Rodaway were restored to the team, and there was a debut for young full back, Steve McAdam, but they could not inspire Burnley to victory. With four games to go, Burnley had to get a point at home to Bristol Rovers on 12 April to have any chance of staying up. A Billy Hamilton goal earned a 1–1 draw in front of a crowd of just 5,270, but it was not enough. Watford had won at Notts County and thus condemned Burnley to the Third Division for the first time in their history.

The decline from a First Division side with potential to one in Division Three had been sudden. It was generally accepted that Burnley had not the resources to compete with the top city clubs, but their failure to make any impact in the Second Division was a grave cause for concern. The main butt of criticism was chairman, Bob Lord. At times of greatest pressure on him he had, on three occasions, dismissed the manager. But these were only cosmetic changes, as on each occasion the replacement came from within the club (the promotion of Joe Brown proved an especially mistaken action). With 2,443 shares out of around 4,000, Bob Lord maintained his all-powerful position within the club, and must therefore take the majority of the blame for the internal decline.

Chapter 6

Indian Summer

(May 1980–2 June 1983)

Relegation ensured a large turnover of playing staff. Free transfers were given to Arins, Burke, Hall, Smith and Richard Overson. James was sold to Swansea City for £130,000; Robinson to Sparta Rotterdam (£35,000); Ingham to Bradford City (£30,000); and, in December, Brennan went to Bolton Wanderers for £25,000. To replace these players, the club bought the Oldham Athletic full back pairing of Ian Wood (free transfer) and David Holt (£45,000); Steve Taylor, the ex-Bolton, Oldham and Luton striker was purchased from Mansfield Town for £35,000; and Tommy Cassidy, the Northern Ireland midfielder came from Newcastle United at a cost of £37,500. Amongst the new apprentices was a promising England Schoolboys international, Trevor Steven.

The new team provided an undistinguished start – a 1–1 draw at home to Newport County. The first victory came the following week, but Burnley could not prevent First Division, West Ham taking a 2–0 first leg lead from Turf Moor in the League Cup. Following this defeat the central defence partnership of Rodaway and Thomson was ended. It was to prove Thomson's last appearance after 12 years at the club; and Rodaway played only twice more before a free transfer to Peterborough at the end of the season. They were replaced by a new combination of Vince Overson and Martin Dobson. Their first two games resulted in two defeats – 2–0 at Charlton (putting Burnley in 20th place) and 4–0 at West Ham. But starting with a home victory over Colchester, the defence did not concede a goal for another 675 minutes of league football – a new club record. Also in this defence were David Holt and Brian Laws, the young right back. Laws had made his debut in the last game of the previous season and was now preferred to the new signing, Ian Wood. In September, a further purchase was made – Eric Potts, a midfield player from Preston North End. He had previously turned down a £50,000 transfer in the close season, but was bought only 3 months later for £20,000. He made his debut in the goalless draw at Chester in a team of:

Stevenson

Laws   Overson   Dobson   Holt

Scott   Cassidy   Potts

Cavener   Hamilton   Taylor

The point put Burnley into 12th place, only two points behind the leaders. The run without conceding a goal included a five-goal defeat of Millwall (with a Steve Taylor hat-trick), but came to an end in early October, when a 3–2 victory over Sheffield United put Burnley into third place. In the FA Cup non-league Scarborough came to Turf Moor and narrowly lost 1–0 (Left back Andy Wharton made his debut as substitute in this game). In the next round striker Mickey Wardrobe played his only full game for Burnley in the draw with Port Vale. Steve Taylor returned for the replay, which Port Vale won 2–0. There was some compensation for Brian Miller, when it was announced that he had won the £1,000 Clarets Lottery (his wife had recently won a TV in the club's Christmas draw).

League form continued well – Christmas wins over Plymouth (2–1) and Blackpool (4–1) kept the Clarets challenging for promotion. In the game against Blackpool, Alan Stevenson was sent off in the last minute, and was replaced for the next two games by Billy O'Rourke. Only six goals were scored in the next eight games, and as Burnley only gained one point off the three teams who eventually went up (Rotherham, Charlton and Barnsley) they lost touch with the battle for promotion.

Stuart Robertson was re-introduced to the midfield and there were debuts for Nelson-born defender Michael Phelan and for Trevor Steven. Steven came on as substitute in a 4–2 win over Huddersfield on 14 April. It was too late to launch a promotion bid and Burnley finished ninth, despite the fact that the defence established a new club record of 21 clean sheets in a season.

There were no new acquisitions for the 1981–82 season (the future Liverpool and Republic of Ireland striker, John Aldridge, who had rejected Newport County's terms, did write to Burnley for a trial, but nothing came of his offer). In the opening game at Gillingham, the defence looked vulnerable and this defeat (1–3) was followed by another – 2–4 at Fourth Division Tranmere Rovers in the League Cup. The second leg at Turf Moor attracted a crowd of only 2,375 – an all-time low attendance at Burnley. A post-war league low of 3,789 for the game with Doncaster Rovers saw the start of a four match losing sequence which took the Clarets to 22nd position – only two places from the bottom.

The board once again came in for much criticism. Before the start of the season, the ground admission price had been raised from £1.35 to £1.90. This increase was largely blamed for the declining gates, although, of course, the team's poor form did not help. Bob Lord had been ill for some time, and in October he announced his decision to sell almost all his shares. He retained 100 in order to stay on the board, but the remainder were sold to a consortium headed by directors John Jackson and Dr David Iven for around £50,000. Jackson, a local barrister, became the new chairman; the admission price was reduced to £1.70 and the concessionary rate re-introduced (£1 for pensioners and under-fourteens). In order to improve the club's image with the local public, a Supporters' Association was formed, and 350 people attended the inaugural meeting at the 'Centre Spot'.

There was also a change on the field of play – Brian Miller went into hospital for an appendicitis operation, and Frank Casper took over the running of the team. Together, they devised a new defensive system, which put Martin Dobson in a sweeper's role. On the left side of midfield, Kevin Young replaced Eric Potts, who was given a free transfer at the end of the season. This left a team of:

Stevenson

Dobson

Laws   Overson   Phelan   Wharton

Scott   Steven   Young

Hamilton   Taylor

This formation worked immediately – goals by Young and Wharton produced a 2–1 victory at Portsmouth. Six of the next seven games resulted in draws – the next win came in late November at Bristol City (3–2 – two of the goals coming from Paul McGee, who was on loan from Preston North End). Another win, over Oxford brought Burnley out of the relegation places in early December. Three days later came news that Bob Lord had died. He had remained chairman for too long in many people's eyes, but his contribution to the club over nearly 30 years cannot be denied.

His influence continued to be felt even after his death. He had recently come to an arrangement with the club over the sale of some of the club's property. Lord had sold a piece of land to the club in the 1960s for £11,000. He tried unsuccessfully to buy it back in 1973, but claimed in 1979 that he was entitled to purchase the land at the original price. The board disputed this and Lord threatened to sue them. An agreement was eventually reached, by which Lord and his family would receive one-third of the proceeds of its sale. They therefore received over £30,000 when the land was sold the following April.

In November, two games were needed to dismiss non-league Runcorn in the first round of the FA Cup and also to beat Bury in the next. A Billy Hamilton hat-trick helped to defeat Altringham 6–1, but 5 days later, Burnley lost 1–0 at Shrewsbury Town in the fourth round. The following week, Kevin Young was sent off at Huddersfield, but two Steve Taylor goals gave Burnley victory. This was part of a six-match winning sequence which saw the Clarets rise rapidly up the table (this was the first season in which there were three points for a win), and by mid-February after a win at Swindon, they were in fifth position. The adoption of the sweeper system with both full backs encouraged to get forward produced a 20-match unbeaten run, which came to an end at Exeter in March.

A bad ankle injury to Steve Taylor caused Miller to sign Brian Flynn on loan from Leeds United, but he was injured in only his second game. Paul McGee was signed on a permanent basis for £25,000 to partner Billy Hamilton up front. In a goalless draw at Wimbledon, Phelan broke a cheekbone and received ankle injuries, which kept him out for the rest of the season and his central defensive role was given to David Holt. Four points were taken off leaders, Lincoln City and a win over promotion-rivals, Chesterfield consolidated Burnley's fifth position with six of their last eight games at home.

A surprising 5–3 home defeat by a ten-man Southend United threatened the surge for promotion, but a 2–0 win over Bristol City four days later put them back on course. Two goals by Billy Hamilton gave victory over Preston North End and put Burnley into second place with only two games remaining, needing a win at Southend on 14 April to gain promotion. They duly obliged – the 4–1 result was achieved through goals by both full backs, Wharton and Laws, and two from Paul McGee. A 1–1 draw at home to Chesterfield, played in waterlogged conditions in front of a crowd of 18,665, was not enough to clinch the title on the night. Burnley had to wait until the following evening – Carlisle United could not score seven, and so, in their centenary season, Burnley became Third Division Champions.

In the close season, Overson, Laws, Steven, Hamilton, Phelan and Wharton all signed new 2-year contracts, which showed the club's commitment to keeping this promising squad together. (Hamilton and Cassidy both played for Northern Ireland in the 1982 World Cup in Spain where Hamilton was outstanding.) Season ticket sales reflected this optimistic mood, nearly reaching the £100,000 mark. Vince Overson was to miss most of the season with a groin injury, and Holt partnered Phelan in the middle of the defence, where Dobson continued as sweeper. Left back Phil Ray made his debut in the opening goalless draw at home to Bolton Wanderers. He was replaced by Wharton for the 5–3 win at Bury in the Milk Cup (formerly the League Cup). Wharton was amongst the scorers along with Scott, Phelan, Steven and McGee. Goals by Laws, Dobson, Hamilton and Young gave the Clarets a 4–1 win at Middlesbrough and left David Holt as the only regular outfield player not to have scored. A further 4–1 victory (over Carlisle United with a Hamilton hat-trick) helped Burnley into fourth place.

A 2–1 home defeat by Rotherham United started a run of four successive defeats, which saw a drop down the table to 18th. This slide caused the abandonment of the sweeper system, and with Dobson back in midfield, Burnley beat Crystal Palace 2–1 at Turf Moor. But three away defeats in a week put them back in trouble. Advertising was introduced on the team's shirts. A deal was negotiated by the new Commercial Manager, Wayne Dore, with the Manchester-based housing firm of 'Poco'.

Tommy Cassidy was recalled to partner Trevor Steven in the centre of a four-man midfield at First Division Coventry City in the Milk Cup. They inspired Burnley to a 2–1 victory, with two goals by Paul McGee, playing alongside Taylor in attack (Hamilton was suspended). A 3–0 defeat at Newcastle put Burnley in 20th position, which finally showed the need to strengthen the squad. The ex-Manchester City left back, Willie Donachie was signed and proved very effective in his debut – a 2–1 win over Cambridge United. The following week, Brian Flynn was signed from Leeds United for £60,000. This purchase meant that the club did not pursue its interest in its former winger, Terry Cochrane. Flynn's first game was at Sheffield Wednesday, where Burnley gained only their fourth away point of the season, but lost Donachie for 6 weeks with damaged knee ligaments.

A 2–1 defeat at Chelsea was described by chief coach, Frank Casper, as 'the worst we've played for two years'. The following week, Alan Stevenson was again sent off – against Leicester City. Burnley were 2–1 up until the sending off, and eventually lost 4–2 (both Laws and McGee missed penalties for Burnley). Billy O'Rourke returned to the team, but could not prevent Christmas defeats by Blackburn Rovers and Wolves, which sent Burnley to the bottom of the table. On New Year's Day 1983, a Steve Taylor hat-trick contributed to a 4–1 defeat of Sheffield Wednesday, but any optimism was soon countered by a disastrous 3–0 defeat at Burnden Park, where Bolton goalkeeper, Jim McDonagh scored the third goal with a kick from his own penalty area. This was the last straw for the board, and the following Tuesday, Brian Miller was relieved of his duties, only 8 months after being named Third Division Manager of the Season. Frank Casper was appointed caretaker manager.

His first game could hardly have been tougher – at Tottenham Hotspur in the quarter finals of the Milk Cup. After the defeat of Coventry in the third round, Burnley had beaten another First Division side, Birmingham City to earn this tie at White Hart Lane. Alan Stevenson was restored to the side, which played out a goalless first half against a Spurs team including internationals Clemence, Hoddle, Ardiles and Villa. When Terry Gibson scored early in the second half it appeared all over, but a 65th minute own goal by Graham Roberts let Burnley back in. Soon after, goalkeeper Clemence was only booked for handball outside his area in a season when some referees would have sent him off. But from the resulting free kick, Billy Hamilton achieved some justice and put Burnley ahead. In the 85th minute, Roberts deflected Taylor's cross into his own goal, and in the dying seconds, a 20-yard effort from Hamilton gave Burnley a famous 4–1 victory and earned a semi-final tie with holders, Liverpool.

At Anfield in the first leg, they looked as if they might repeat the shock. Twice before half time, Derek Scott was clean through – his first effort struck Grobbelaar, the keeper, on the head, and the second in the 37th minute, hit the outside of the post when it looked easier for him to score, and Burnley's chance was gone. Four minutes later, Souness' shot deflected off Flynn into the goal, and further goals in the second half by Neal and Hodgson gave the Merseysiders a three goal lead to take to Turf Moor. In the return in front of a crowd of 22,550, Scott did manage to score – in the 54th minute. A minute later, Lawrenson was forced to clear his own misplaced tackle off the Liverpool goal-line to remove any doubt as to the outcome. The 1–0 defeat was their first in 15 games, but it was nevertheless, Liverpool who went through to the final.

Burnley were also making progress in the FA Cup. A replay was needed to dismiss Carlisle United in the third round, but one game sufficed to beat Fourth Division, Swindon Town. A goalless draw at Crystal Palace meant a replay at Turf Moor, which Burnley won 1–0. The goal came from a penalty in the 83rd minute – Laws missed the initial kick, but the referee adjudged that Fry, the Palace keeper, was off his line. Steve Taylor drove the retaken kick straight at Fry, who had obligingly dived out of the way. This technique was noted by Jack Charlton, manager of the sixth round opponents, Sheffield Wednesday. Burnley were awarded a penalty in only the 5th minute of the game at Turf Moor, which Taylor duly hit at Wednesday keeper, Bob Boulder, who stayed upright and saved the kick with ease. The crowd of 23,134 then saw Wednesday dominate the first half and they scored when Gary Banister punished Dobson's hesitation. Burnley came back well in the second half, and gained a headed equaliser by Tommy Cassidy in the 46th minute. A semi-final with Brighton beckoned for the winners, and in the replay, Wednesday were two goals up within half an hour. A harsh penalty in the 42nd minute, given against Donachie, effectively sealed the tie. Two further goals after the break completed a demoralising 5–0 defeat.

The cup runs had attracted attention away from the fight for Second Division survival, but league form had not suffered. A fifth away point was obtained at Rotherham, and home victories over Barnsley, Charlton Athletic and Fulham lifted Burnley out of the relegation positions. Against Charlton, both Hamilton and Taylor scored hat-tricks, and a superb solo effort by Trevor Steven rounded off a 7–1 victory, which helped earn Casper the Second Division Manager of the Month award for February. Taylor's place in the side was threatened by the purchase of Terry Donovan from Aston Villa for £25,000. He made his full debut against Newcastle United in March, and scored the only goal of the game.

However, following the FA Cup defeat at Hillsborough, league form began to deteriorate and although almost £250,000 had been obtained from the cup runs, Casper was unable to make any more purchases before the transfer deadline. With 13 matches left, eight were away from home. Burnley had still only won away once in the Second Division (they had won twice on First Division grounds!). Their poor form continued in a lethargic defeat at Cambridge, which started a losing sequence of five matches, including defeat at Blackburn – a game marred by crowd trouble. The game had to be halted for 14 minutes following missiles thrown on to the pitch by rioting Burnley fans. Billy Hamilton's two goals inspired a home victory over Chelsea, but two mistakes by Alan Stevenson meant a 2–0 defeat at Derby. Stevenson equalled John Angus' post-war record of 438 appearances for Burnley in this game, but was dropped for the following one at Shrewsbury. A 25-yard drive from Phelan and a goal by Donovan were enough to give Burnley a much-needed victory. Champions QPR were beaten by two more goals by Donovan and a goalless draw was obtained from the penultimate game at promotion-chasing Leicester City. This left Burnley needing to win the last game at Crystal Palace, who themselves required a point to stay up. In a strangely lack-lustre game, Burnley could only muster one attempt on goal – and that in the 80th minute from substitute Vince Overson when the Clarets were already a goal down (Overson, who had started just one game all season, had been sorely missed).

The position of Frank Casper was still unclear. Despite the two cup runs and a brave late effort to avoid the drop, the club once again found itself in Division Three. The last five managerial appointments had all been made from within the club itself and the board, therefore, decided to break with this tradition. On 2 June 1983,

John Jackson announced, 'We have considered all the circumstances including the results over the past four years in which we have been relegated to the Third Division twice, and we have made the policy decision to appoint an outsider.'

1981–82 – Division Three

Back: Holt, Phelan, Cassidy, Hamilton, Stevenson, Overson, Dixon, Taylor, Dobson
Front: Steven, Laws, Young, Scott, Wharton, McGee

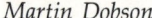

Martin Dobson

John Bond

Martin Dobson and John Bond. Dobson had two spells at the club: he was signed in 1967 by Harry Potts and sold to Everton for £300,000 in 1975. He came back in 1979, and finally left the club in 1984 when the manager was John Bond. Bond was manager for just one season (1983/84) but the effects of his reign were felt for a long time after his departure. (Photographs © The Burnley Express)

Chapter 7

John Bond and After

(14 June 1983–9 May 1987)

The outsider chosen was John Bond. He had most recently been at Manchester City, taking them to the 1981 FA Cup final, and had also enjoyed success at smaller clubs, Bournemouth and Norwich City. He brought in John Benson as his assistant, which meant there was no place for Frank Casper.

It had already been arranged to sell Trevor Steven to Everton, and this deal brought in £350,000 for the new manager to spend. Roger Hansbury, the ex-Norwich keeper, was brought from Hong Kong to replace Alan Stevenson, who went to Rotherham United on a free transfer. Joe Gallagher, an experienced central defender was purchased from West Ham for £35,000. A trio of ex-Manchester City players came to the club: Tommy Hutchison, 35, who had also been playing in Hong Kong; Gerry Gow, a tough midfielder who was bought from Rotherham for £15,000; and Kevin Reeves, only 25, an England international signed for £1 million only a few years before, was purchased for £100,000. The influence of the charismatic Bond obviously helped in these acquisitions. 'I would not have gone down to the Third Division for any club unless it was managed by John Bond,' said Hutchison, who was made the new club captain in preference to Martin Dobson. Bond did not enhance his local reputation when he sold another popular player, Brian Laws, to Huddersfield Town for £20,000. Laws had missed only ten games during the previous three seasons, but on the evidence of the pre-season games, Bond reached the conclusion that 'although he is quite good going forward, I do not believe he is a good enough defender'. Of the players freed at the end of the previous season, Tommy Cassidy went to Cyprus, Steve Taylor to Wigan and Paul McGee became player-coach at Sligo Rovers. A Newcastle United bid of £150,000 for Hamilton was turned down. Season ticket sales of £76,500 reflected a guarded optimism, shared by the club's bankers, the TSB, who became the team's new sponsors.

The season began badly – a 4–1 defeat at Hull and a Milk Cup exit to Crewe, who had finished in 91st place the previous season. 'What amazes me,' claimed the manager, 'is how simple the solution is – to get better players. Once I have got that team together, I will take full responsibility for what happens.' Turf Moor regular, Kevin Young, was replaced by Gerry Gow for the opening home league game with Bournemouth. This made a team of:

Hansbury

Scott   Overson   Phelan   Wharton

Hutchison   Gow   Flynn   Dobson

Hamilton   Reeves

The change worked. A Hamilton hat-trick helped towards a 5–1 victory. A further win over Newport County three days later took Burnley into eighth position.

John Bond was still not satisfied with his squad. He was interested in Cardiff full back, Linden Jones, and Sunderland central defender Shaun Elliot, but the asking prices of £70,000 and £120,000 respectively proved a stumbling block. A Burnley bid of £15,000 for Jones was turned down, and the board put a limit of £100,000 on the manager for Elliot. John Jackson, the chairman, was prepared to fly to Seattle in an attempt to get Steve Daley on a free transfer. The ex-Manchester City midfielder, who had previously been bought for £1,437,500 was involved in contractual difficulties, which delayed the deal for some months. A central defender was eventually obtained, when Malcolm Waldron was signed from Southampton for £85,000.

At Turf Moor, Burnley won all but one of the games before Christmas. Seven goals in 49 minutes against Port Vale in November put them into sixth place. But away they struggled – the first win coming on 17 December at Wimbledon, where on John Bond's 51st birthday, a 4–1 victory ended the London club's 25-match unbeaten home run. Earlier in the month, both Bond and Benson signed contracts to keep them at Burnley until the end of the 1985–86 season. 'The future looks a lot brighter now,' said Bond, 'It would take something exceptional to remove us from this football club now.'

Steve Daley was finally purchased for £20,000, and he was joined by another ex-Manchester City player, Dennis Tueart, picked up on a free transfer from Stoke City. Tueart became the seventh full international on Burnley's books alongside Dobson, Donachie, Flynn, Hamilton, Hutchison and Reeves. Bond defended his decision to buy another experienced player by saying, 'You can't get young quality players on free transfers. So if you want quality, we have got to go for the older players. Dennis is a good player – and that's all that matters.' He started well – scoring on his debut in the 5–0 defeat of Scunthorpe United on 31 December. A 2–1 win at Orient three days later kept Burnley in touch with the leaders.

Having knocked non-league Hyde United and Chesterfield out of the FA Cup, Burnley were drawn at home in the third round to Oxford United. A goalless draw at Turf Moor was followed by a 2–1 defeat at Oxford. Roger Hansbury was struck by a coin during the game, but a more serious injury affected Kevin Reeves. Severe hip trouble meant that Reeves had to miss the rest of the season. His loss was keenly felt by the side, especially by his striking partner, Billy Hamilton, who had already scored 17 goals – many of these from Reeves' near-post flicks at Brian Flynn's corners. Terry Donovan had been transferred to Rotherham United in September, so as a replacement, John Bond turned to Wayne Biggins from Matlock Town. He scored in only his second game (4–0 vs Exeter) and in his fourth he netted a hat-trick against the club that had discarded him, Lincoln City (4–0). Hamilton, however, lost his goalscoring touch and scored only four times after Reeves' injury.

The side was still on the verge of the promotion race in March, but this did not satisfy the manager. 'Our main problem is in mid-field,' said Bond, 'I have never got it right all season and until I can, we cannot operate properly.' A severe blow to the midfield was the loss of Martin Dobson. He was tempted away by Bury's offer of a player-managership, and played his last game for Burnley on 10 March in the goalless draw at home to Bristol Rovers. His replacement was David Miller, son of the ex-manager, who had made his debut earlier in the season and was now given an extended run in the team. Another departure was that of Malcolm Waldron who went to Portsmouth for £60,000. Due to the consistency of Overson and Phelan, he had been unable to establish himself in his normal central defensive position and he had been played in various positions including right back, where Bond never adequately replaced Brian

Laws (Lee Dixon, the future England international, was also given a free transfer by Bond). A full back was finally obtained, when Steve Baker was signed on a month's loan from Southampton. Bond was unable to add more to his squad. He believed that he had got Chesterfield winger Alan Birch on loan, but Birch was sold to Rotherham United just before the transfer deadline, leaving the depleted squad to challenge for promotion.

Two goals by Wayne Biggins provided 1–0 victories over Millwall and Gillingham in late March, but two similar setbacks over Easter at Newport and Bournemouth ended the promotion hopes. Bond had obviously given up for the season, and now spent his time watching other games, trying to build a squad for the following campaign. A Steve Daley hat-trick at Port Vale on 28 April gave Burnley their first win for 2 months, and four consecutive defeats at the end of the season ensured a disappointing 12th position.

Before the start of the season, due to the £600,000 raised from the cup runs and the sale of Trevor Steven, the club's financial situation had stabilised, which allowed Bond to spend much of it in the transfer market. It was revealed in the club's financial statement that £419,605 had been spent on transfers. Due largely to the sale of Steven, a profit of £4,195 was made, but much of the money was wasted. As director, Derek Gill said: 'too many players did not justify their fees'. Joe Gallagher was plagued with injury problems and played only nine times, the same number as Gerry Gow who was released; Steve Daley left the club to go to America, having had a disappointing season; and another of Bond's signings, Malcolm Waldron, was never given a fair chance to prove his worth. On the plus side, Hutchison and Hansbury were ever-present, and Reeves formed a very effective partnership with Hamilton before his unfortunate injury, which finally forced him to retire from the game. He was appointed youth team coach, whilst Hamilton was unwilling to carry on in the Third Division, and was transferred to newly-promoted Oxford United in exchange for ex-Bolton striker, Neil Whatmore and £80,000. Willie Donachie and Kevin Young were both given free transfers. Donachie went to Second Division, Oldham Athletic, and Young, who had played only twice for Burnley all season and had had spells on loan with Torquay and Port Vale, teamed up with Martin Dobson (and Frank Casper) at Bury. Another departure was the sponsor, TSB, who pulled out after a year, although a new agreement was negotiated with 'Multipart'.

In an attempt to rebuild the squad, Bond made six new signings: Peter Hampton, ex-Leeds and Stoke full back; Neil Grewcock, a winger from Shepshead Charterhouse; Peter Devine, from Blackburn Rovers; Alan Taylor, who had scored twice for West Ham in the 1975 FA Cup final, now released by Hull City; Barry Powell, an experienced midfielder now playing in Hong Kong; and Kevin Hird, a local born full back from Leeds United, who could also play in midfield.

After the failures of the previous season, the chairman was concerned over all this activity in the transfer market, which led to Bond issuing a statement – 'All I want to do is manage the club in my own way as I have done at my previous clubs. But I am afraid that it is an impossibility for any manager when there is friction between himself and the chairman.' This sounded to the chairman like an ultimatum, and at a board meeting on 20 August, 5 days before the start of the new season (1984–85) Bond was dismissed and John Benson put in charge of team affairs.

For the opening game – a 1–1 draw at home to Plymouth Argylle – the team lined up:

Hansbury

Scott   Phelan   Overson   Hampton

Hird   Powell   Hutchison

Grewcock   Taylor   Biggins

As in the previous season, Burnley suffered a Milk Cup first leg defeat by Crewe (1–2), although they came back well to win 3–0 at Crewe. In the second round, they were drawn against First Division, Manchester United. The first leg at Old Trafford was only eleven seconds old when Bryan Robson put United into the lead and a Mark Hughes hat-trick sealed the victory. A 3–0 defeat for Burnley at Turf Moor in the second leg merely emphasised the gulf between the two clubs.

Despite a poor managerial record, John Benson was confirmed in the position and the side struggled in the league. At Rotherham, Derek Scott broke his leg and was out of the team for nearly 5 months. Phil Malley, who had made his debut in the final game of the previous season, came in at right back. Only two wins in the first 11 matches put Burnley in 18th position. Benson described the

2–1 home defeat by Lincoln City as 'the worst display I have seen a Burnley side give since I came to the club. It was pathetic.' The following week, they lost 5–1 at Reading, despite leading at half time. The introduction of Whatmore for Taylor at centre forward made little difference. Whatmore scored only once in nine appearances and he was transferred to Mansfield Town in March after several months on loan. The continued good form of Billy Hamilton at Oxford left few in any doubt as to who had got the better of that exchange. During the season, four new centre forwards were tried, and this still proved an inadequate replacement for the one sold.

The situation was improved by a 3–1 win over Brentford, but only 2,915 turned up to see it – a new low post-war league gate at Turf Moor. There was some relief in the FA Cup, where hat-tricks by Hird and Taylor helped Burnley to a 9–0 win over Penrith, which equalled the club's highest ever score, and broke the record 7–0 away win. Brian Flynn was dropped following the defeat at Reading, and he asked for a transfer. In November, he went to Cardiff City for £20,000. This allowed Benson to bring in two new players: Les Lawrence a centre forward from Rochdale for £15,000; and Geoff Palmer, an experienced full back from Wolves for £5,000.

It was clear that Benson had nothing like the spending power of his predecessor. In November, the club announced a loss for the previous year (up to 31 May 1984) of £112,515 – this would have been more but for the £114,500 compensation for Reeves' injury. The disappointing 1983–84 season was reflected in a drop of £200,000 in match income. Chairman John Jackson admitted the failure of the John Bond era, though he defended his decision to appoint an outsider – 'the greatest part of the disaster,' he said, 'was due to lack of judgement in its implementation rather than an inherent fault in the policy.'

After the cup victory at Penrith, the next seven league games produced only one point and sent Burnley down to 20th position. Only in the FA Cup was there victory, a 3–1 win over Halifax at Turf Moor with goals by Hird, Biggins and debutant Peter Devine. This set up a third round tie at Wimbledon – 10 years after their last cup meeting. But now Burnley were the underdogs and lost 3–1 to the Second Division side. The first goal was caused by Hansbury's error and after the game he asked for a transfer. As a replacement, Joe Neenan was brought in on loan from Scunthorpe United. In his first game – a 5–1 victory in the Freight Rover Trophy against Stockport

County – he drew applause from the crowd merely for shouting at the defence. In his first league game, he had little to do as a hat-trick by Hird, two goals by Biggins and one each for Devine and Lawrence gave Burnley a 7–0 win over Rotherham. Steve Kennedy had been re-introduced to the defence, allowing Phelan to play in midfield. Unfortunately Kennedy suffered a knee injury in the next game and the impetus was lost. As in 1982–83, a seven-goal tally in February had little effect on the struggle against relegation.

Neenan's loan period was renewed for another month, but moves to make the transfer permanent were foiled when Scunthorpe asked for £25,000, which they knew Burnley had just received from Everton. Trevor Steven had just been capped by England, and this payment was part of the 1983 transfer deal. Burnley were unwilling to spend the whole sum on Neenan as the club was suffering financially. Cost-cutting measures included the sale of part of the Gawthorpe training ground, and the Commercial Manager, Wayne Dore, was made redundant. Hansbury was restored to the team for the 1–1 draw with Bournemouth in mid-March – a result which put Burnley into the relegation places. A deal to swap Derek Scott, the new club skipper, for Bolton winger Jeff Chandler foundered on Scott's unwillingness to move, and the only newcomer was Rotherham's Mark Rhodes, who had been substitute in his team's 7–0 defeat at Turf Moor.

A dreadful performance at Wigan (0–2) on Easter Monday put Burnley only two places off the bottom. Two goals by Alan Taylor against Cambridge United the following week gave the first victory for 11 games, but four days later what Benson called 'a pathetic joke' of a performance led to a 4–0 defeat at Bristol Rovers. For the remaining three home games, the board halved the ground admission price to £1 in order to 'bring in extra support to give the team the will to avoid relegation'. Nevertheless, only one point was gained from these games, making a total of 26 points at home out of a possible 69. Away from home, they fared better. Tommy Hutchison starred in a 1–0 win at fellow-strugglers, Swansea City, now managed by John Bond. In the last game of the season at Walsall, two goals by Taylor and a scorcher by Kevin Hird meant that if Swansea lost the following Friday, Burnley would stay up.

It was ironic that the club's fate lay in the hands of John Bond. The disunity in the boardroom which his appointment (and dismissal) had caused could be seen in the events of that time. Before the game at Walsall, John Jackson had resigned as chairman, although he intended to stay on the board. His expected successor, Derek Gill, the club's managing director, did not take over and announced his own resignation the following week. 'I have to state,' he said, 'that I would not accept the position of chairman of a board comprising the current members. Before this club can recover, failed and incompetent individuals must be removed.' Two days after Gill's resignation, Swansea obtained a goalless draw at the Vetch Field against Bristol City, and Burnley were relegated to the Fourth Division for the first time in their history.

John Benson's contract was terminated 'by mutual consent' and the manager's job was advertised. Frank Teasdale, who had only been on the board since January, became the new chairman and received 62 applications for the post. The man chosen was Martin Buchan, 36-year old ex-Manchester United and Oldham Athletic defender, who had no previous managerial experience. Scott and Phelan refused new contracts and both left the club. Phelan was transferred to Norwich City for £70,000 and after over 10 years at Burnley, Scott felt he was no longer wanted and moved to Bolton Wanderers for £20,000. Buchan's first signing was Joe Neenan, signed on a permanent basis to replace Roger Hansbury, who had gone to Cambridge United on a free transfer (David Miller, also released, went to Tranmere Rovers). Tommy Hutchison was offered a coaching position at Burnley, but preferred to rejoin Bond at Swansea. Reeves, too, left the club, and was replaced as youth coach by Joe Gallagher. Buchan's other signings were central defenders, Ray Deakin from Bolton and Jim Hegarty, from Larne in Northern Ireland.

Tommy Cavanagh, the former assistant manager at Manchester United, was brought in to help with training and pre-season games went well. Wayne Biggins scored hat-tricks in victories over Rochdale (7–0) and Bolton (4–0) in the Lancashire Manx Cup. The highest crowd in the Fourth Division (4,214) saw Burnley race to a 3–0 half-time lead against Northampton Town at Turf Moor in the opening game of the season (1985–86). In the second half, two goals by Northampton left the Clarets hanging on for victory. Two home defeats followed and a Milk Cup knockout at the hands of Martin Dobson's Bury. A Wayne Biggins goal gave victory over Rochdale, but Joe Neenan received a fractured jaw in a clash with Steve Taylor. Dennis Peacock was picked up on loan from Doncaster Rovers, as a replacement and started well in a goalless draw at Peterborough.

This was followed by two defeats in five days – 2–0 at home to Colchester and 4–0 at Chester, where the visiting supporters jeered their team off at half- and full-time. 'It was suicide,' acknowledged Buchan, 'a feeble performance.' He was not satisfied with his own performance as manager and after only 110 days in the job, he resigned. 'I could not make the transition from the dressing-room to management' he admitted. Team affairs were put in the hands of Tommy Cavanagh.

Cavanagh's first two games in charge resulted in two more defeats and Burnley slipped to 17th position. They also lost the services of Wayne Biggins, who was sold to Norwich City for £35,000 (plus £5,000 when he had played twenty league games). Neil Grewcock, too, almost left the club to go to Bolton Wanderers – the clubs agreed a fee of £10,000 but personal terms were not reached. Burnley had already signed another striker – Derrick Parker, who had played five times for the Clarets in the First Division, came from Oldham Athletic for £10,000. A 3–1 home defeat by Southend United marked the end of Peacock's unhappy loan spell. Phil Harrington was signed on loan from Blackpool and played in just two games – both victories – including a 4–0 win at Cambridge United against Roger Hansbury. Neenan returned for the FA Cup tie at non-league Nuneaton Borough where Burnley won 3–2 thanks to a last minute goal by Peter Devine. This earned a match at Rotherham, where Burnley were comprehensively beaten (4–1).

League form continued to improve. An own goal and two penalties against Exeter produced a win, which took Burnley into 11th place. This was improved with another home victory over Orient. Ashley Hoskin, an Accrington-born winger, who had made his debut at Cambridge, suffered a fractured leg in only the 2nd minute, and after only six games he was out of the game for 3 months. Orient's Sitton was sent off for the foul, and the opponents were reduced to ten men. This was repeated in the next two home games – Comstive of Wrexham and Carter of Hereford were the offenders. Two victories (5–2 and 3–2, respectively) helped Burnley into the top eight, but any hopes of promotion were dashed by two away defeats – at Hartlepool and at Torquay, the bottom club.

The season petered out tamely. Only 1,961 turned up to watch a home defeat by Crewe in April. The following week a draw at Preston ensured that North End had to seek re-election for the first time in their history, thereby showing the general decline of the Lancashire town clubs. Vince Overson had had enough and announced his intention to quit the club. He was warmly applauded off the field when substituted in the 80th minute of the 2–1 defeat by Scunthorpe at Turf Moor. Overson was signed in the close season season by John Bond, now at Birmingham City, for £25,000 (plus 50% of the profit on any resale). A 2–2 draw at Colchester in the last game of the season meant that Burnley finished in 14th position.

The club's poor financial position required urgent attention. Negotiations took place with a group of local businessmen, including Derek Gill, but the board refused Gill's conditions, which were reported to be himself as chairman and the appointment of Martin Dobson as player-manager. The club was within 24 hours of calling in the receiver, when it got an offer of assistance, which meant that the bank could guarantee the club's future for another season. It also led to the introduction of three local businessmen as new directors – the addition of Bernard Rothwell, Bob Blakeborough and Clive Holt produced a seven-man board. John Jackson had sold the vast majority of his shares to Frank Teasdale, and the previous March had resigned from the board.

The bank had insisted on economy measures: the club decided that its reserve team would not seek re-election to the Central League; and they were forced into releasing both Kevin Hird and Alan Taylor. Hird went to Colne Dynamoes in the Second Division of the North West Counties League (with the guarantee of a job outside the game), and Taylor joined the large ex-Turf Moor contingent at Bury. 'We simply could not afford to renew their contracts,' said Cavanagh. Cavanagh himself went into hospital for a hip operation and on his return announced his resignation 'for medical reasons'. He was quickly replaced by the ex-manager, Brian Miller, who had been running a newsagents' shop. Miller chose as his assistant, Arthur Bellamy, and was told that he could pick up three or four new players on free transfers. His first two signings were players he had managed before. Leighton James, now 33 came from Newport County to start his third spell with the club; and Billy Rodaway was released by Tranmere. Another ex-Claret rejoined the club when Jim Thomson became the new Commercial Manager.

Miller also made two loan signings: Ian Britton, the ex-Chelsea midfielder from Blackpool; and striker Wayne Entwistle from Bolton. Joe Gallagher, who had not played in the first team for 18 months and had been fighting against medical advice to retire, was re-introduced into central defence to partner Ray Deakin, the new club captain, following Overson's departure.

An away draw at Torquay was followed by a 1–0 victory over Scunthorpe at Turf Moor with a penalty by Leighton James. James, combining well with Hoskins, inspired a victory at Wolves and a further win – 3–1 over Halifax – put Burnley into fifth position in late September. Two goals by Tranmere's Ian Muir, who had had a spell on loan at Turf Moor in 1982, halted Burnley's progress and a pathetic display losing 4–1 at home to Preston shattered any illusions about promotion.

Further defeats at Northampton (2–4), Exeter (0–3) and Cambridge (1–3) dropped the Clarets to 17th position, and they entered the FA Cup tie versus non-league Telford United as underdogs. Burnley became the tenth league side that Telford had beaten in the previous five years, but the saddest aspect of the 0–3 scoreline was not so much the result, but the lack of surprise at it.

In desperation, Miller turned to the youngsters at the club on the YTS scheme. Peter Leebrook, 18, at right back and Jason Harris, 16, in midfield made their debuts in a fine 3–1 win over Lincoln City. Darren Heesom made his first appearance of the season, and there was a goal on his debut for Phil Murphy, a striker formerly with Blackpool. The year ended on a high note with a 4–0 win over Crewe, but 5 days later, on New Year's Day 1987, Burnley crashed 3–0 to bottom club, Rochdale.

Joe Neenan missed the next game with a calf injury, which meant a debut for Tony Woodworth. It proved a disaster, as Burnley went down to the biggest post-war league defeat at Turf Moor – 6–0 to Hereford United – and Burnley were in 21st position. Neenan returned for two 2–2 away draws at Hartlepool (where the Clarets were 2–0 up with 12 minutes remaining) and at Swansea (where Ashley Hoskin scored a memorable solo goal). The defence, however, did not improve – 2–1 up at half time against Wolves at Turf Moor, Burnley lost 5–2. A centre forward, Mark Caughey, holder of two Northern Ireland caps, was signed on loan from Hibernian and he was partnered up front by Ian Britton, who was moved forward for the rest of the season. Four consecutive draws maintained Burnley's 21st position. An Ashley Hoskin goal against Stockport gave Burnley their first victory of the year (13 March) and this was quickly followed by a good 2–1 win over runaway leaders, Northampton Town. But four consecutive defeats plunged Burnley right back into trouble –

only one from the foot of the table in the first season of automatic relegation from the Football League for the bottom club.

There were now only eight matches left – the next two against fellow-strugglers. Burnley were very lucky to obtain a 2–2 draw against Torquay United at Turf Moor with a last minute penalty by James. At Rochdale, however, they ran out deserved 2–0 winners, which put them five points off the bottom. In front of a crowd of 5,379, over half from Burnley, the scorers were Phil Devaney, an 18-year-old striker in only his second game, and Joe Gallagher.

Defeats at Cardiff and Scunthorpe coupled with Rochdale's improved form took Burnley to the bottom of the division, one point behind Torquay and Rochdale with only three games left – two at Turf Moor where Burnley had won only once in 1987. Southend United took the lead, but a magnificent 25-yard drive from Leighton James and a second half effort by Neil Grewcock were enough to give the Clarets victory and took them off the bottom. But after a midweek loss at Crewe, they entered the last game back in 92nd position.

To survive in the Football League, Burnley had to win their last game at home to Orient on 9 May, and either Lincoln or Torquay had to drop points. It looked to be no easy task, as Orient were still pushing for promotion. Out of desperation, the directors wrote to the Football League claiming that the automatic demotion of the bottom club was 'both unfair and inequitable'. They cited the facts that Burnley were founder members of the League and had, as far as they knew, never had to seek re-election. The letter also mentioned Burnley's fine stadium and above average attendances and hoped that the Fourth Division could be extended to 25 clubs irrespective of which club finished bottom. A similar plea from a Burnley fan had already met with a refusal from League Secretary, Graham Kelly, who had said, 'Although it would be indeed a tragedy to lose a founder member, I am sorry to say that it is too late to change the rules now.' There is no reason to suppose that the Burnley board's request would have provoked a different response.

Chairman, Frank Teasdale pronounced that the 'game is without doubt the most important Burnley have ever played'. There was widespread sympathy for the club's predicament. Good luck messages were received from almost every league club in the country, and the public responded to the plight of the club, rather than the present team, which as captain Ray Deakin pointed out, had 'given no-one any reason to come'. A crowd of 17,600 made its way to Turf Moor – over three times the season's previous highest and around six times higher than the average attendance. Jimmy McIlroy spoke for many, when he admitted that 'for the first time ever at a football match, I felt my eyes moist. This was my club on the brink of humiliation.' The Burnley line-up on this momentous occasion was:

Neenan

Leebrook   Gallagher   Deakin   Hampton

Grewcock   Rodaway   Malley   James

Devaney   Britton

The kick off was delayed for 15 minutes to let all the crowd get in, which gave Burnley the advantage of knowing that the other results were going their way – both Lincoln and Torquay were losing.

Orient were in no mood to be intimidated by the large crowd and only a goalline clearance by Peter Leebrook in the opening minutes stopped them from taking the lead. It was the visitors who created the best chances in a tense first half – Godfrey struck a post and Cornwall hooked the ball over the bar from a promising position. However, in the last minute of the first half, Neil Grewcock cut in from the right wing and scored with a shot from 20 yards. Ian Britton headed a second just 3 minutes after the interval and Burnley appeared safe. But, 8 minutes later, Alan Comfort scored for the Londoners to set up a nerve-wracking last 34 minutes. Another good chance fell to Cornwall, but his shot struck Phil Malley rather than the back of the net and Burnley hung on to their lead. Lincoln had lost, Torquay only drawn and so Burnley had survived, much to the relief of the Turf Moor crowd, and also to the many thousands of exiled Clarets' fans listening to the live commentary on national radio. The scenes after the game were strongly featured on the television news, as many of the crowd spilled onto the pitch to celebrate the victory in which they had played a vital part. 'I shall never quite determine who won the match,' wrote Ian Wooldridge, one of the many national newspapermen at Turf Moor to cover the match, 'the Burnley team or the crowd.' One young fan, quoted in the local press, had a different suggestion – 'I've been praying all week we would stay up,' he said. 'I believe in God now.'

It was a memorable end to a near-disastrous season, where Burnley finished in 90th position. Had they dropped just one more point, then they would have dropped out of the Football League – the same league that they had topped 27 years previously. The small step to footballing obscurity had been avoided, and Burnley, one of the founder members of the Football League, had survived to take part in its centenary season.

Chapter 8

The Road to Wembley

(10 May 1987–29 May 1988)

Despite the poor season, the club's financial position had been improved. The board obtained the backing of the bank and announced plans to strengthen the playing side. The scouting system was reintroduced, as was the reserve team, although an application to join the Central League was turned down. Leighton James was appointed as youth team coach, whilst remaining available for the first team. There was a large turnover in playing staff. Besides James, only seven players (Leebrook, Deakin, Britton, Malley, Devaney, Grewcock and Hoskin) were retained. Joe Neenan refused terms, was sacked by the club and given a free transfer. He was replaced by Chris Pearce, signed from Wrexham along with midfielder Paul Comstive for a combined fee of £12,000. Striker George Oghani and defenders Peter Daniel, Peter Zelem and Shaun McGrory were picked up on free transfers, whilst young midfielder Andy Farrell cost £5,000 from Colchester United. The pre-season games, including a morale-boosting victory over Blackburn Rovers, also saw the debut of central defender Steve Gardner, a non-contract player freed by Manchester United.

The season proper began disappointingly with a 3–0 defeat by Colchester and a 1–0 defeat in the Littlewoods Cup first leg match at Wrexham. Miller once again plunged into the transfer market to re-sign Steve Taylor from Preston North End for 'a small fee'. Steve Gardner was also signed on a permanent basis. This meant that nine players had been signed for a total of less than £20,000. The first win of the season was achieved at Newport with the team:

Pearce

Leebrook   Zelem   Gardner   Deakin

Daniel   Farrell   Comstive

Grewcock   Oghani   Taylor

The good form continued with a 3–0 victory over Wrexham in the Littlewoods Cup (earning a second round tie with First Division, Norwich City) and a 4–3 home win against Carlisle United. There was a setback at Leyton Orient (1–4), but three consecutive 1–0 victories, all achieved with late goals, saw the Clarets top the Division they had so nearly dropped out of only 4 months before.

Wayne Biggins and Michael Phelan returned to Turf Moor with Norwich in the Littlewoods Cup. Burnley's revival was underlined as they gained a 1–1 draw, in which Biggins equalised Oghani's early goal. Burnley produced another good display in the second leg, but went down to a Mark Bowen goal. Despite the defeat, the performances helped restore much pride and confidence to the club.

League form proved inconsistent. A 3–1 win at Torquay in late October kept them in third place, but consecutive defeats at Halifax and Wolves sent them down to 11th position. An FA Cup defeat by Bolton Wanderers was avenged the following week by a 2–1 victory with Ian Britton and David Reeves as the Burnley scorers. Reeves, a 20-year old striker, had been signed on loan from Sheffield Wednesday. Another loan signing, central defender Steve Davis, was now signed on permanently from Crewe Alexandra for a fee of £15,000. Burnley met up again with Joe Neenan in November, now playing for Peterborough United. He had a quiet afternoon, as his team achieved a 5–0 victory. Defeat at Cardiff on the Saturday before Christmas put the Clarets in the bottom half of the division.

In the Freight Rover Trophy victories over Tranmere and Rochdale meant a home tie with Third Division, Chester City. Steve Davis totally subdued Chester's prolific goalscorer, Stuart Rimmer, and the game was settled by Oghani's 80th minute goal. Burnley faced another Division Three team, Bury in the next round of what was now re-named the Sherpa Van Trophy. A Paul Comstive goal earned them a well-deserved victory at Gigg Lane in February. David Reeves was signed on a third month's loan and his goals in wins over Darlington, Colchester and Exeter City helped Burnley back up the table into fourth place at the beginning of March. Unfortunately, his loan period could not be renewed. Reeves had proved a valuable asset to the Burnley team. For the previous two home games, double-priced turnstiles had been set up in order to raise money for purchasing players and £6,037 had been collected. But Sheffield Wednesday, now struggling in Division One, refused to contemplate selling Reeves. Such was his loyalty to Burnley that he announced his intention not to go to another Fourth Division club on loan that season.

Another loss to the attack came in the first half of the Sherpa Van Trophy northern semi-final against Halifax Town at Turf Moor, where a leg injury to Neil Grewcock was to keep him out for the rest of the season. The tie itself remained goalless through extra time, which necessitated a penalty shoot-out. The first six penalties were converted successfully (Deakin, Hoskin and Britton were the home scorers). Halifax keeper, Paddy Roche got a hand to George Oghani's effort but could not prevent Burnley going 4–3 up. Roche himself took the next penalty, and his shot struck the bar. Paul Comstive then made no mistake – his fiercely-struck spot-kick put Burnley into the northern final against Preston North End.

In the league, the loss of both Reeves and Grewcock proved insurmountable. Three wins in the final 11 games was obviously not promotion form and the team finished tenth, but attention had long since turned to the Sherpa Van Trophy. Victory over Third Division Preston in a two-legged tie would mean Burnley's first visit to Wembley since 1962. A goalless first leg at Turf Moor in front of a crowd of 15,680 seemed to favour the visitors, especially as the second leg would be played on Deepdale's artificial surface, where Preston had won ten of their last 12 fixtures.

Burnley trained on the pitch on the previous evening and adapted well to the surface – George Oghani's 17th goal of the season put Burnley into the lead, but Gary Brazil's equaliser sent the game into extra time. The first period was only 3 minutes old when Ashley Hoskin scrambled in a goal following a goalmouth mêlée, and a further goal from Paul Comstive, 3 minutes from time, settled the issue and sent the Burnley fans in the 17,592 crowd into ecstacy. From near-oblivion the year before, their team was now going to Wembley.

Burnley's opponents in the final were Fourth Division Champions, Wolverhampton Wanderers. In the Football League's centenary season it seemed fitting that two of its founder members were to meet at Wembley. Both sides were enjoying something of a revival, and the game on Sunday 29 May attracted a crowd of 80,841 – more than had seen the previous week's England v Scotland international. The two sets of supporters mingled happily together outside the ground, savouring an occasion which showed many of the positive aspects of the game.

Steve Gardner had picked up a knee ligament injury in the last league game of the season, but passed a late fitness test to make the team:

Pearce

Daniel   Davis   Gardner   Deakin

Britton   Farrell   Comstive

Oghani   Taylor   McGrory

Wolves had already inflicted two 3–0 defeats on Burnley that season. They were put into the lead by Andy Mutch in the 22nd minute, and six minutes into the second half went further ahead following a superb free kick by Robbie Dennison. Leighton James replaced McGrory after 62 minutes, and on his eighth Wembley appearance he sparked a Burnley come-back. Twice Paul Comstive headed against the bar and he had a further effort cleared off the line. But the Clarets did not score, and Wolves ended the game strongly and came close to adding to their lead.

The 2–0 defeat did not seem to affect the enthusiasm of the Burnley fans, and 20,000 greeted the team on their return the following day, including 8,000 at Turf Moor. The trip to Wembley had restored the town's pride in its football club. A quote in the local press summed up much of the local feeling – 'I support Burnley Football Club,' proclaimed one fan, 'We may not be the greatest team in the Football League, but we are, without any doubt, the greatest club.'